Praise for
The How-To of Great Speaking

*"The Persons Method is both simple and effective.
It's helped me enjoy public speaking."*

**—Stewart S. Nagler, Senior Vice President,
Metropolitan Life Insurance Company**

"This is a great book—the best I have read on the topic."

—Peter Economy, Director of Administration, Horizons Technology, Inc.

*"Thanks to learning your presentation skills
I'm a much better trainer. You teach people to be themselves.
You helped me enhance who I am.
And, I am much better at being myself than anyone else."*

—Jude Heimel, Trainer, AT&T Bell Laboratories

*"No one can surpass Hal's expertise in developing public
speaking skills that in turn build personal poise and
confidence. He has created a remarkable methodology
and is a master at teaching it."*

—Richard Gottlieb, President, Executive Strategy Group

*"The ability to communicate is critical in today's international
business environment. Hal Persons' methods may be humorous
and simple but the effect is quite serious and sophisticated.
Best of all, [the methods] are devastating to those butterflies
and delightful to audiences."*

—Jim Ferri, Senior Vice President, Hill & Knowlton

"The Persons Method is a unique application of stage techniques that has improved my business communications through the use of fundamental acting skills. Must reading for anyone in business who needs to communicate effectively."

**—Thomas Watson, President/CEO
Diversified Agency Services, Omni Group, Inc.**

"I am a committed believer in Hal Persons' teaching method and the principles he sets forth in this book. My successful career in advertising is based largely on the fact that Hal turned me into a confident and dynamic speaker."

—Jacqueline Silver, Research Consultant and President, J. Silver, Inc.

"Your book is terrific! Your techniques helped me become more at ease when talking to an audience. What you talk about is what I experience as a musician. For example, your presentation/performance flow chart is a very good prescription for a successful piano solo."

—Dick Hyman, Concert pianist and orchestra conductor

"The Persons Method is a highly effective vehicle for building public-speaking skills. Learning to speak before a large audience without notes has allowed me to become a more sincere and confident speaker."

**—Midge McGraw, Director of Labor Planning and Policy Development
State of New York, Department of Labor**

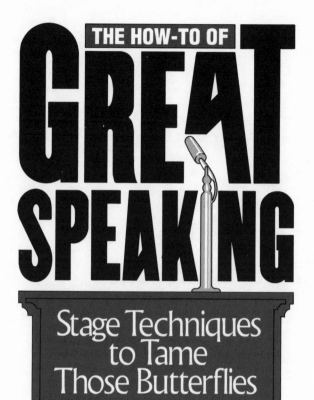

THE HOW-TO OF GREAT SPEAKING

Stage Techniques to Tame Those Butterflies

Hal Persons
with LIANNE MERCER

FOREWORD BY JACK LEMMON

A BARD PRODUCTIONS BOOK

Black & Taylor
PUBLISHERS

Printed in the United States of America

Library of Congress Cataloging-in-Publication Data

Persons, Hal, 1918–
The how-to of great speaking: stage techniques to tame
those butterflies / Hal Persons with Lianne Mercer.

p.   cm.
Includes index.
Trade paperback: ISBN 0-9632786-0-6
Hardcover: ISBN 0-9632786-1-4
1. Public Speaking.   2. Voice culture.
I. Mercer, Lianne S.   II. Title.
PN4121.P38   1991
808.5′1—dc20   90-41040
                                          CIP

Black & Taylor Publishers
5275 McCormick Mountain Drive
Austin, Texas 78734
512/266-2112 Phone
512/266-2749 Fax

A BARD PRODUCTIONS BOOK
Editing: Alison Tartt
Illustrations: J. Kay Wilson
Text Design: Barbara Jezek/Suzanne Pustejovsky
Production: Barbara Jezek
Composition: Round Rock Graphics

This book is dedicated to William Shakespeare, the world's first acting and speech teacher.

"*I should like to depart from my prepared text and speak as a human being.*"

CONTENTS

FOREWORD

Hal Persons' book starts by telling the reader . . . "Speaking is a natural skill which a person begins to develop in the first year of life." However, with most of us that natural skill gets deflected off course in many directions, before (if we ever do) we can learn to use that skill to its fullest advantage for ourselves . . . hopefully without offending or boring our listeners. Persons shows us how to develop the necessary discipline to stay on course, how to ensure ourselves and our audiences that when we speak we have something to say . . . even more important, something the audiences want to hear.

A few of the most important items covered are:
- Home work. This includes knowing what the basics are of your potential audience—age group, professional identification, interests to at least some small degree. Quite obviously, also, your home work has to include total knowledge of your subject.
- A conscious effort to impress or intimidate will not work—you need to identify with the individuals who have come to hear you, to have confidence in their ability to relate to you just as you relate to them.
- Speak clearly so that you can be understood.
- Speak with enthusiasm and maintain as much eye contact with individuals as you possibly can.
- Use visual aids as *assistance*—don't become just a "pointer."

Most of all, read and enjoy Hal Persons' book—and then, if you truly want to be an expert speaker, STUDY it and learn from it.

—Jack Lemmon

PART ONE

THINKING ABOUT SPEAKING

1

WHY THIS BOOK

You're holding the key to the most effective performances of your life right here in your hands. You'll learn to say . . . what you want to say . . . the way you want to say it . . . at the time you want to say it.

Speaking is a natural skill which a person begins to develop in the first year of life. Yet according to several surveys, speaking in public is what people fear most.

How about you? Where do you rank public speaking on your list of fears? I have a good idea—after all, you're reading this book!

Why do you fear speaking in public? Perhaps for two very good reasons.

First, especially if you're in business, pressure to speak well is overwhelming. The *Harvard Business Review* (January-February, 1964) states that "a person's ability to communicate is a primary consideration in selection for promotion to management." An AT&T survey (AT&T Information Systems ad, *Business Press*, 1985) shows that 85 percent of a white-collar worker's day is spent in verbal communication.

According to a *Training and Development Journal* article, (September, 1980) human resource development professionals in Fortune 500 companies believe that "improving communication is the most important training topic for executive, middle, and supervisory management."

I want to repeat what I said in the first paragraph: speaking is a natural skill which you began to develop in the very first year of your life. So your fear of public speaking is cause for great concern because it's unnecessary. Sad to say, that fear has been taught to you by some very well-meaning people. And that's the second reason you probably fear speaking in public.

The How-To of Great Speaking takes away the artificial superstructure placed by pedagogues on the simple, natural function of speaking. It returns you to the basics.

This book is written for anyone for whom talking is an important part of his or her job—anyone who needs to inform, persuade, or inspire. It evolved out of over twenty years' experience teaching effective speaking skills to more than 35,000 executives, many from Fortune 500 companies.

I use a time-tested method—the approach used by professional speakers since before Shakespeare. It is based on the teaching method developed by Constantin Stanislavsky, the famous prerevolutionary Russian director. "The method"

Oh, there be players I have seen play—and heard others praise, and that highly—that neither having the accent of Christians, nor the gait of Christian, Pagan, nor man, have so strutted and bellowed that I have thought some of nature's journeymen had made them and not made them well, they imitated humanity so abominably.
—William Shakespeare, *Hamlet*

fosters natural, believable, and charismatic performance and is based on the use of improvisation and storytelling.

The Persons method is based on two imperatives:

- Be yourself
- Tell 'em whatcha wanna tell 'em

The Persons method shows you *how* to be yourself and *how* to tell 'em whatcha wanna tell 'em. It's been proven, perfected, and polished for over 20 years. Most of the how-to skills are physical and can be learned through practice. You'll feel what it's like to successfully use these techniques in practice so you can use them masterfully where it counts— in front of an audience.

The Persons method shows you how to improve your business communication by exploiting such fundamental acting skills as diction, projection, delivery, timing, winning an audience, and conquering stage fright. You'll learn to use methods perfected by professional speakers: actors, announcers, emcees, lecturers, and entertainers.

The Persons method doesn't intend to qualify you to become an actor. But it stands to reason that these professionals have developed techniques invaluable to the business executive.

(When I say "actor," I'm not being sexist. To the professional, there is no such thing as an actress. Katharine Hepburn calls herself an actor. It's a generic term. So when I say "actor," please understand that I'm talking about all four sexes.)

The *How-To of Great Speaking* is basic. It will demonstrate that being an effective speaker is simple. However, it is not a "quick and easy" method, though the benefits will begin immediately. It is not instant mashed potatoes. It isn't a book of platitudes.

Most manuals on speaking are full of technical terms and jargon which alarm rather than enlighten. I'm not going to do that. I'm going to enlighten. I'm going to tell you how to do it. Most public speaking courses give you a crutch. I'm going to show you how to walk on your own two feet. I use the common experiences of people to teach you *how*

The greatest charm of (nineteenth-century actress) Anna Cora Mowatt's manner is its naturalness. She speaks and moves with a well-controlled impulsiveness as different as can be conceived from the customary rant and cant, the hack conventionalism, of the stage.
—Edgar Allan Poe, quoted in *Backstage with Actors*

Beware of jargon—it can lead to talking about acting taking the place of actually doing it.

Although there is no lack of material about all aspects of (Shakespeare's) plays and stagecraft, most actors feel that this does not really help them as actors. One of them once showed me a Shakespearean Grammar he had got hold of in the hope of getting his bearings. It was a daunting document, full of technical terms which alarmed rather than enlightened.

—John Barton,
Playing Shakespeare

to accomplish your objectives. You'll laugh. You'll find it interesting. You'll find it easy to do.

A fortunate amalgam of business, educational, and theatrical skills gave birth to the Persons method. I've directed television shows on NBC, CBS, and Mutual; had years of experience directing, acting in, and stage-managing Broadway shows, national touring shows for the Shubert organization and summer stock companies; taught verbal communications skills at Columbia University Graduate School of Business, the American Institute of Banking, and York and LaGuardia colleges; and conducted a successful professional theater school, the Theatre Academy of Long Island.

The knowledge I garnered from these myriad sources is helping thousands of business speakers by taking the hell out of making a presentation, teaching a class, or preaching a sermon.

There will be no footnotes in this book, because I can't remember exactly who taught me which of my trade skills. I've had at least ten acting teachers, three speech teachers, and several dance instructors. I've worked with maybe a hundred different directors. I've discussed acting with countless professional actors, and I've read hundreds of books on all phases of theater.

That's not unusual: the same is true of every dedicated actor and director I've known. A true theater professional is a very culture-oriented person who has a broad knowlege base in practically everything. In the old days, actors were mostly self-taught. Until well into this century, most actors had only an elementary formal education. Shakespeare never took Lit 235 or Psych 101.

Some of what I learned came from my teachers, who had been in turn inspired by Edwin Booth, Eleonora Duse, George Bernard Shaw, Edmund Kean, Sarah Bernhardt, David Garrick, Cicero, and Aristotle. And my method is heavily influenced by the teachings of Constantin Stanislavsky with an assist from William Shakespeare. I cannot begin to remember all the techniques inspired by my pupils at the Theatre Academy.

Many things I taught, which I thought were original, had

been thought of by others. For years I'd been using a technique to help aspiring actors. Then I found that it was coincidentally part of another technique used by John Barton of the Royal Shakespeare Company. He works a good three thousand miles from New York City. We've never met.

The Persons method is an expert method designed for busy executives. So often an expert is a person who'll tell you more about something than you need to know. I'm telling you just what you need to know. I realize you're a busy person, so I've arranged this book in four progressive sections that you can complete in small blocks of time. Within each section, you can easily retrieve the information.

I've designed this method so you can select your own time to work on it. You don't have to carve out a block of time from your busy schedule. You can practice some of the techniques while taking a shower, mowing the lawn, driving a car, or attending a party.

You're holding the key to the most effective performances of your life right here in your hands. You'll learn to say *what you want to say, the way you want to say it, at the time you want to say it.*

Let's begin.

You cannot eat the turkey with one bite. First you take one bite, then another bite, and before you know it the turkey is consumed.
—Constantin Stanislavsky, *An Actor Prepares*

2

THERE'S A METHOD TO CONTROL THIS MADNESS

If you're typical, you'd rather undergo an appendectomy than stand up and speak before a group. You are subjecting yourself to needless agony. There's a method to control your madness.

Frank, that was an excellent presentation.''

"Great talk, Suzanne.''

"Henry, this has been the best class I've ever attended.''

Substitute your own name because it could be you they're complimenting. It's easier than you think to earn that figurative pat on the back and, best of all, to know in your heart that you did well, that you're a winner.

If you're typical, however, you'd rather undergo an appendectomy than stand up and speak before a group. You are subjecting yourself to needless agony. There's a method to control your madness.

Reprinted with special permission of NAS, Inc.

IT'S A PROVEN METHOD

The method is not new. It's based on over five hundred years of experience by professional speakers: actors, entertainers, lecturers, and after-dinner speakers.

You see, when most people talk, it's a tool. They use words as they'd use a computer terminal, a screwdriver, a frying pan, or a broom. Most people use words to accomplish something. Words are a tool.

But when the professional (the actor, the emcee, the lecturer) talks, words are the product. And we have to talk so well that people like you are willing to *pay* to hear us. If you've been to the theater lately, you know it's an enormous expense. Besides purchasing tickets, you have to pay for a babysitter, parking, and dinner, plus an apre-show drink. So unless the professional is good, he or she doesn't eat.

It stands to reason that a method has been developed to

help the professional to be as good as he or she is capable
of being.

NOW LET'S DEFINE THE MADNESS

Why is it that you and so many other intelligent people would
rather wrestle a lion than make a presentation?

Professionals have known the reason for centuries
because we have a sure-fire criterion. If it sells tickets, it
works. If it doesn't . . . .

Our experience has been corroborated by a book written in recent years called *The Book of Lists* by David Walle-
chinsky, Irving Wallace, and Amy Wallace. Now if it's in
a book, it's got to be true, right? It's an interesting book.
Some six hundred pages of the ten most-married men, the
fifteen most disastrous battles, and so on. (One page even
lists the ten most popular positions in sexual intercourse. I
would tell you the page to save you the trouble of looking
it up, but someone tore that page out of my copy and pasted
it over my wife's mirror.)

Now get this. In the list of fourteen things people fear
most, number seven on the list is the fear of dying. *Death*
is number seven!

Do you know what humankind's number one fear is?
I'm sure you're way ahead of me. It's the *fear of speaking
before a group*.

Since back way before Shakespeare, professional speakers have known about this phenomenon. We call this number
one fear *stage fright*.

So if you would rather undergo surgery or go over
Niagara Falls in a barrel than get up before a group, there's
nothing wrong with you. You are typical. That should be
of great comfort.

You've Done It To Yourself

Experience has taught us that this phobia is mostly a self-
imposed state.

Do you remember as a child the terror of entering a dark

*Just returned from see-
ing Edmund Kean. By
Jove, he is a soul!
Life—nature—truth,
without exaggeration or
diminution.*

—Lord Byron, quoted in
Backstage with Actors

room? The terror of going down into the basement? You were afraid of the bogey man, of the monster, of the vampire. Today, you know that these threats are nonexistent. By and large, the monster most people fear—an audience out to get you—does not exist!

Professionals know that the majority of an audience, by its very nature, is extremely courteous and will give you every break. Should you forget a word, people will supply it. They'll supply acronyms, names, and locations. If you happen to overturn a pitcher of water, there might be some tittering, but it will be sympathetic. They'll probably be saying to themselves, "There but for the grace of God go I—another member of the Klutz Club."

Ninety-five percent of the time, an audience is courteous, understanding, and interested in your point of view, even if some people in the audience disagree with you. Hostility and skepticism do exist, especially if you are in the public sector—government or utility corporations. This book will deal with even the exceptions in due course. Just remember, most of the time, audiences consist of people just like you—people you meet in the cafeteria, on the elevator, and in the library. But even if you have never met them before, you must understand that they put on their shoes one at a time just like you do. They wash; they get hungry; they cry.

When you have conniptions about being in front of them, you're putting yourself through needless hell.

But to tell you not to be afraid is like telling a tooth not to ache. It doesn't work. You've got to get to the root of the problem.

But first, why should you care? Why should you want to be an interesting speaker? For two very good reasons.

First, you spend most of your time speaking with other people. An AT&T ad in the September 1985 issue of *Business Press* states that 85 percent of a white-collar worker's day is spent communicating: attending meetings, talking on the phone, conducting interviews, sending requisitions, answering questions, handling complaints, and explaining and indoctrinating.

Think of it! You actually get to move a project from Position A to Position B only 15 percent of the time. The rest of the time, you're *talking* about moving it.

Second, your ability to communicate effectively influences how fast and how far you're promoted. In a survey reported by the *Harvard Business Review* in January, 1964, under the qualifications management considers important for promotability, the ability to communicate effectively was listed not only once but three times.

So let me summarize. You—along with most other people —are caught in this self-imposed madness: you know that a large part of your job and your future depends upon your speaking ability, and that scares you to death!

Take Comfort: You Know How To Talk

The first thing you have to understand is that you *do* know how to talk. When you get down to it, talking is no big deal. You were born with the ability to talk. You began talking beautifully somewhere between the ages of one and two, or even earlier. You said clever things; you were observant; you were poetic; you were humorous. And if you don't believe, ask your mother. You were a veritable genius.

Why is it, then, that you, a successful, enterprising achiever who was born with the natural ability to speak, would rather join the French Foreign Legion than get up in front of a group and tell them what you know about a subject in which you're an expert?

But You've Been Conditioned!

One of the reasons that too many business people speak badly is that they have been conditioned to speak badly. If you've ever taken a public speaking course, your instructors didn't teach you to be natural, to relax, and to say things in a simple, unassuming way.

No way.

You've been given the impression that in order to get up before a meeting you've got to become a combination of Abraham Lincoln, Winston Churchill, and Sarah Bernhardt rolled into one. Somehow, to talk about the demographics of Detroit, you've got to be transformed into a deity standing on Mount Olympus throwing down lightning bolts of pure, unadulterated wisdom in every syllable.

That's a crock! Trying to achieve that unattainable image is what makes so many speakers uptight and therefore brittle and boring.

If you'll think back to all the great speakers or teachers you've enjoyed, they were natural, weren't they? They were witty. They were personable. They were lovable.

They were human. They were human. They were human. And because of that, their message stuck with you.

And don't underestimate lovable. We read practically every day of one legislator who gets away with murder while another in the same party who does the same thing gets slam-dunked. Lovable can make a big difference.

And You've Been Given Too Many Rules

No good actor is bound by any rules. It's absurd to say there are any set formulas for acting comedy or tragedy—one set of gestures the actor pulls out of a hat when he is a clown, another when he is a tragic figure. What you do and how you do it depends entirely on the play and the part you portray.

—Alfred Lunt, quoted in Famous Actors and Actresses on the American Stage

Has delivery style been defined? No. But teachers constantly try. Does one of the following scenarios sound familiar?

Here's how one public speaking class listed step one for a question-and-answer session:

> Project confidence nonverbally. You want to project a professional image to correspond with your delivery style.

How's that again? How do you do it? You can't possibly do step one because you haven't been taught *how to* achieve and project confidence nonverbally. You haven't been taught *how to* achieve and project a professional image to correspond with your delivery style.

A scene from the other end of the "rules" spectrum might go like this. You are the speaker. The audience has come to hear you talk about "The Psychological Implications of Peanut Butter on International Commerce." That's the message. That's what's important.

But that message becomes secondary because you're worried about your speech coach's rules on how to deliver that message to the audience. You're worrying about things like the following:

1. Keep your jacket buttoned.
2. Keep your feet ten inches apart and parallel.
3. Keep your hands at your sides.
4. Scan the audience with your eyes.
5. Talk loudly.
6. Talk slowly.
7. Talk with expression.
8. Be warm.
9. Be sincere.
10. Be enthusiastic.
11. Smile.

Then the coach says, "Relax!"

How can you?

Actors know how to do all the above, not by using numerous rules, but by using a few basic techniques of human behavior. In fact, some of the concerns implanted in the above list (such as buttoned jacket, feet planted, hands by your sides) are not even necessary or desirable.

Such arbitrary concerns are one of the principal causes of stage fright. Actors *do* get stage fright.

KNOW THE ENEMY

Let me tell you about stage fright. Stage fright can render geniuses incapable of remembering their own names. Stage fright can cause war heroes who faced bombs and bullets to faint dead away when they have to get up and talk.

Stage fright can cause you either to hide behind the podium or to hide behind a wall of words. You get stiff because you don't look at the people you're talking to; you deny yourself human contact. You feel isolated.

You see, it's not natural to be the only one talking. In everyday communication, I say something, you say something, I say something. But, remember, even when you're the only one speaking, if you play off your audience, you're

Edmund Kean's first appearance at Drury Lane was as Shylock. At home in the evening, as he was leaving for the theatre, he told his wife, "I wish I was going to be shot."

—Helen Ormsbee,
Backstage with Actors

going to get instant feedback. It's just that most of the feedback is nonverbal. You will essentially be having a dialogue and no longer feel isolated. We'll talk more about how important feedback is and how to obtain it in a later chapter.

Another reason stage fright strikes is that you're afraid of making a fool of yourself by appearing unskilled and unprofessional. Let me remind you that you're an intelligent person. (You bought this book, didn't you?)

You've got to assume that when the company hired you, it didn't do you a favor. You have worth because most companies are not philanthropic organizations. Too often, not even philanthropic organizations are philanthropic to their employees. Your company believes you're knowledgeable, or your boss wouldn't have asked you to make that presentation to the chairman of the board. Your company hired a talented individual. Not a number or a face in the crowd. Unless, of course, your father owns the company.

From the time that first Greek stomping on the grapes in the circle drank some of the grape juice, got a little inspired, and stood on a rock to perform that lewd dithyramb, actors have been working on methods to overcome stage fright.

This book is based on that methodology, handed down for thousands of years from generation to generation.

HERE'S THE METHOD IN TWO PHRASES

There's one rule I have on stage, and that is that I will never let myself get away with the phoney.
—Anne Bancroft, quoted in
Actors Talk About Acting

Let me tell you in two phrases how easy it is to be a star platform speaker.

First, *be yourself.*

When I say be yourself, I'm talking about your *natural self*! Without veneer. Without facade. Unpretentious. Unposed.

I am talking about the self you reveal to your closest buddy, sitting in your living room with perhaps a glass of distillate of grain in your hand. *That* self!

That's phrase number one: *be yourself*!

Phrase number two: tell 'em whatcha wanna tell 'em! In other words, tell it like it is.

You have information to impart. You want your audience to do something. Talk to the people at the meeting as if you're talking to your closest friend. Perhaps to your parents. Perhaps to your brother. Perhaps to your sister or to your children.

Tell them what. Tell them why.

Tell 'em whatcha wanna tell 'em! is phrase number two.

These two phrases are the essence of excellent speaking.

When you have mastered the ability to be natural, when you are able to talk simply and directly, when you are fearless, *you'll* be in control.

You will be able to say

What you want to say,

The way you want to say it,

At the time you want to say it.

The rest of this book is devoted to telling you how to accomplish this goal.

> **What you must dare is to be yourself.**
> —Dag Hammarskjold,
> *Markings*

> *Speak the speech . . . as I pronounced it to you, trippingly on the tongue. But if you mouth it . . . I had as lief the town-crier spoke my lines . . . use all gently; for in the very torrent, tempest, and, as I may say, the whirlwind of passion, you must acquire a temperance that may give it smoothness . . . Be not too tame neither, but let your own discretion be your tutor . . . hold as 't were, the mirror up to nature.*
> —William Shakespeare,
> *Hamlet*

PART TWO

PREPARING YOURSELF TO MAKE A WINNING PRESENTATION

3

HOW TO RENDER YOURSELF ARTICULATE

Public speaking, like athletics, is highly physical. You can't wish proficiency. You've got to develop the muscle to coordinate what you say with what you're thinking.

Just like everyone else, you can make a great speech in your mind.

On the way to the meeting you know you will be able to make a devastatingly precise evaluation of the situation as well as to recommend solutions, parry objections, and handle questions.

On the way home you know exactly what you should have said.

But at the meeting you wondered, "Why is my voice so high-pitched? What is my hand doing up in the air? Why am I clutching the podium?" You allowed misstatements to go unchallenged. You nodded approval when you really disapproved. When you voiced your impassioned philosophy, it somehow sounded sophomoric. You found it difficult to coordinate what you really wanted to say with the words that actually came out of your mouth.

Too often there's a wide disparity between knowledge of what is necessary and the ability to perform it physically. Just as you cannot wish a winning game of tennis, you can't wish a good presentation. Don't, as many people do, wait for the actual performance, hoping for the miracle that will lead to the inspired performance you see yourself doing in your mind's eye. When it comes to physical skills, miracles just don't happen.

In our imaginations we all can play a great game of golf or tennis. But when we actualize our fantasies, they often fall short of our dreams.

Spontaneous or inspired acting—meaning that something which drops from the sky at the moment when the player, Heaven help him, is on the grill in front of an audience—is equally unreliable. By a miracle it might save an actor once. But it would be unfair to tempt fate twice.
—Katharine Cornell, quoted in *Famous Actors and Actresses on the American Stage*

SPEAKING IS A PHYSICAL PROCESS

You'll soon discover that public speaking, like athletics, is highly physical. And you can't wish physical proficiency. You've got to develop the muscle.

Be comforted. Just as you can learn athletic skills through a series of exercises, you can learn speaking skills. It's easier to be a good speaker. Don't forget, speaking is a natural attribute. What you need to know is how to render audibly what you think in a way that will stimulate audiences. What you say must be coordinated with what you want to say—with what you are thinking.

This is what I call rendering yourself articulate.

Have you ever stopped to think of the remarkable skill of play-by-play television sports announcers? They tell you what's happening on the field. They cite names and numbers of players involved. They describe uniform colors; give interesting sidelights about the history of the game, the players, and the record book; mention weather conditions and the size of the audience; manage a joke or two. All these things are interspersed without seeming to pause for breath and are charming as hell.

Now that's what I call being articulate, yet men like Frank Gifford, John Madden, and Don Meredith acquired that skill through training. Most of them began as pretty inarticulate athletes, whose interviews were a series of "Uh . . . uh . . . uh," "y'know," and "er . . . er . . . er." You, too, can train yourself to be articulate, to say what you want to say, the way you want to say it, at the time you want to say it.

DO SOME CALISTHENICS

I'm going to give you a series of exercises to perform to develop verbal skills. You're going to perform communication pushups. At first they may seem irrelevant to your problems as a speaker, but compare them to the calisthenics used by athletes to develop various performance muscles.

You've seen pictures of boxers hitting a punching bag or skipping rope. Do they actually do those things in the ring? Of course not! They are developing coordination between eye and muscle response. The suggested verbal exercises in this chapter are to develop coordination between what you want to say and what you actually do say.

I'll start with very general warm-up exercises, but I'll progress throughout the book to the nuts and bolts of being a great platform speaker. Don't try to save time by skipping to the final chapters. Work in the suggested order. Remem-

If we haven't any control, we do a thing spontaneously, instinctively, and it's fine, it lasts for a little while; but then if we have no fundamental knowledge of how we did that—we don't know how we did it . . . You acquire this fundamental knowledge by taking yourself apart in every way: you learn your voice, you learn about every note of your voice and just where to place it for certain things. This sounds so terribly mechanical, and it is . . . it's like tennis: you've been playing tennis and you can whack at the ball and get it over the net wonderfully, but if you ever want to get into playing really good tennis, what do you do? You have a teacher come and he just destroys your whole game for a while and you get very discouraged and you can't do a thing—and yet all the time you are learning exactly the snap of the wrist and the use of the shoulder and the follow-through of the stroke.

—Helen Hayes, quoted in Actors Talk about Acting

ber, this is an adaptation of the method of training profes-sionals for the stage, television, and night clubs. It's geared for nonactors, for busy executives, teachers, and others who have to talk for a living.

I'll start with a warm-up. Why? It helps depressurize you from the stress of moment-by-moment living, gives you the proper mind set for what's to follow, and helps dissolve that "cellophane wrapper" too many of us wrap ourselves in.

DISSOLVE YOUR CELLOPHANE WRAPPER

Let me explain what I mean by "cellophane wrapper."

Watch a number of adults as they walk and as they talk. Some are so vibrant and their facial expressions are so open and bright that they seem to be relishing every moment, to be really enjoying themselves. Their faces look alert, their eyes shine, their walk is spritely, and their gestures are enthusiastic.

Then there are the others. Their faces are expressionless or strained, their gait is usually shuffling, and their posture is poor. There is a beautiful, exciting world around them—the same world experienced by the open people—but they don't see it. Their eyes are turned inward.

I see the latter group as having wrapped themselves in an unneeded cellophane wrapper, protecting themselves from heaven-knows-what.

Have you ever noticed in the gourmet section of your food store a white pegboard from which is suspended glassene bags of succulent-looking cashew nuts, apricots, and maca-damia nuts? They look beautiful, but, as attractive as they are, they are untouchable, unreachable.

To which group do you belong? Does the world see the inner you? Or are you, as attractively as you are groomed, going through life looking unreachable and wrapped in cellophane?

Both groups of people started on equal footing when they were children. Stop to observe children between the ages of one and ten. Not every child is beautiful, yet what pleasure we derive from just looking at them, at their open faces, their eyes drinking in every experience, animated, enthusiastic, curious.

Think once again of speakers you've really enjoyed listening to. Weren't they like the enthusiastic first group, like the children? Without exception, I'll bet they were warm, exciting, and youthful. What makes former president Ronald Reagan such an excellent speaker is his warm, youthful delivery. He looks at you. He smiles. He never seems to be making a speech. He is in his mid-seventies, and he deals with serious issues, yet he isn't boring.

For the Reagan-Carter debate in 1980, Reagan had actor training; Carter must have studied public speaking. In the Kennedy-Nixon debate, Kennedy appeared natural, youthful, and charming. Nixon, like Carter, must have studied public speaking. President Eisenhower hired actor and director Robert Montgomery to train him in platform skills. Ike was a great person, but he wasn't projecting his true image.

Not all of us are born with the physical characteristics of a fashion model. But every last one of us has the potential to be an exciting, charismatic speaker. It starts with shucking off that cellophane wrapper.

Take Rex Harrison, for example. He looks like such a natural actor . . . When he comes on stage it looks as if he does just what comes into his head, whereas he's really a most careful, meticulous worker.
—Rita Gam, *Actress to Actress*

LET'S GET STARTED

The warm-up is your self starter to get your motor going, to dissolve the cellophane.

Take your time. Do everything deliberately.

The warm-up is only the first part of each session. After that, you'll read out loud. Then you'll do a verbal exercise. Do each several times, adding detail to each subsequent performance. Each time you repeat, you'll learn the technique of self-editing, which will condition you to have more selfconfidence and therefore render you more articulate.

For best results you should devote between thirty and fortyfive minutes daily to a session. But since this course is designed for the busy executive, give each session as much time as is practical for your schedule. Do each exercise at least two times. To begin with you may feel self-conscious, but you'll soon find that you are enjoying yourself!

Acting is like sex. You should do it, not talk about it.
—Joanne Woodward, quoted in *Actress to Actress*

SESSION 1

Warm-up

Begin your warm-up with something you do every day: in an imaginary bathroom, wash your hands without props.

See the soap and the soap dish; pretend to wet your hands; pick up the soap; use it. Pay attention to details. How thick is the soap? How does it smell? How do you pick up the towel and wipe your hands? How do you hang up the towel? Do you fold it or do you just throw it on the rack?

Do this several times. Remember, each time you must add realistic detail. You're conditioning yourself to be more articulate.

Read Out Loud

Pick an article from a newspaper or magazine, or choose a portion of a novel.

This is especially useful for people for whom English is a second language, or for anyone who needs to speak in another language. Reading aloud is very helpful. People who can understand what they are reading too often are not confident about how to pronounce the words. It's a matter of getting used to hearing yourself say them. Once again, it's a matter of muscular coordination.

Reading aloud teaches you syntax. It teaches you grammar. It teaches you usage.

To help you read more fluently, use the guide for marking a script for sight-reading on page 166. Broadcasters use this method to help them sight-read. Another way of training your ear for correct pronunciation, syntax, and usage is to listen to news broadcasters. They are schooled to speak standard American English. Listen to the news, of course, but pay particular attention to the way the words are pronounced. We've all learned our language by hearing it spoken. Now use the same system to learn to speak it well. If you're unhappy with a regional accent, use this way, nature's way, to correct it. Don't be afraid of change; don't be afraid that people will notice the improvement. In short order, they will forget your old pattern.

Verbal Exercise

If possible, work this section with a tape recorder.

Select an object in the room—a lamp, chair, or table. Describe it out loud. Don't think about what you're going to say; just talk. Don't hesitate. Keep going even if you stutter. Think of the play-by-play announcer. Do not allow "dead air." Fill in as much detail as you can. How high, color, texture, large, small, nice, ugly, you like, you don't like, old, new. Start from the top and work to the bottom.

Listen to the tape. Check your observations as you play it back. Did you leave any details out? Do it again. Try to fill in more detail. Check yourself again.

Do this four or five times.

Here's an example:

1. *First description*: I'm looking at a red cup and saucer. It's made of glass. It's got liquid in it. It's sitting on a table.
2. *Second description*: The glass in the cup is an eighth of an inch thick. There are a few little vestiges of towelling around the outside edges of the cup. The liquid inside the cup is dark brown. The saucer underneath is four inches wide and half an inch deep. Some of the liquid has spilled into it.
3. *Third description*: A narrow ribbon of smoke rises from the hot liquid. The glass of the cup reflects the light into a pattern on the wall. The red color darkens where the cup rests on the saucer.

One of seven children, boxing champ Sugar Ray Leonard grew up in poverty. "A lot of people think I come from a middle-class background, but I started from the bottom," he says. "They tell me, 'Anyone who speaks as well as you do had to have come from a good neighborhood.' "

Leonard is a high-school graduate, but behond that, it was his drive for self-improvement that was critical in developing his language skills. "I used to practice reading from a magazine before a mirror," he explains, "so I could learn good grammar and enunciation and get out of the slang of the streets— from the dis and dats and Wha's happenin', man. I knew if I was going to be more than just a fighter, I'd have to learn the language."

—Ira Berkow, New York Times

SESSION 2

Warm-up

Pretend to pour yourself a cup of coffee and drink it. Pay attention to detail. How thick is the cup handle? How do you pick up a spoon? How do you add the cream and sugar? How do you handle the hot liquid?

Read Out Loud

Follow the directions in Session One.

Verbal Exercise

Describe a picture of a person in the same way you described the lamp or the chair.

You can use a photograph or a picture in a magazine. As in the previous session, use a tape recorder, then listen and check yourself. Repeat and fill in more details. You may begin to add your impressions and perhaps an anecdote inspired by what you see. Get used to the sound of your voice.

SESSION 3

Warm-up

Pretend to pack an overnight bag for a trip. You must try to visualize an actual bag. Do you lay out your things on a bed or a chair, or do you pack from drawer to bag? How do you fold the various articles of clothing? Do you put your toilet articles in first or last?

Read Out Loud

Follow the directions in Session One.

Verbal Exercise

Go to a window and describe what you see happening as though you were a play-by-play announcer or a newscaster describing the scene. Talk about the people you see: describe what they are wearing; comment on their walk, their posture, and their gender. Do you know them? Use anecdotal material perhaps. Discuss traffic. Describe the trees and fences (what type?), the road (unpaved or paved with what material?), road signs, birds, and animals.

Listen to yourself. Then do it again and again.

SESSION 4

Warm-up

Pretend to hang a picture on the wall. Make it a fairly large picture. Is it heavy? Hammer in a nail or hook. Is the picture level?

In the repeat performance, besides looking for more detail, add drama: have difficulty mounting the picture, drop a nail, hit your finger, or have difficulty in leveling the picture.

Read Out Loud

Follow the directions in Session One.

Verbal Exercise

Turn on the television to a sporting event, a parade, or a fashion show. Turn off the sound. Do the running commentary.

ADVANCED SESSIONS

More Challenging Warm-ups

- Make scrambled eggs and toast.
- Get dressed, beginning with your underwear.
- Carve a turkey.

More Challenging Reading

- Read selections from Shakespeare
- Read narrative poetry.
- Read from the Bible.

More Challenging Verbal Exercises

- Set up a game of chess or checkers and play both sides. Verbalize what you are doing; voice your options as well as the reaction of your opposition (which is you, of course).
- Play any board game (like Monopoly), but be all the players. Verbalize as in the checker game.
- Play every hand of a card game. Speak your thoughts as above.

Any actor who is worth anything will tell you that he learns more about the art of acting by watching people than anything else.

—John Strasberg, quoted in
The New Generation of
Acting Teachers

4

HOW TO CULTIVATE YOUR VOICE

The beautiful voice you began life with is essential to your good grooming. Learn to cultivate and enrich that voice by exploiting nature's way of pronunciation and by using proper breath-support and voice placement techniques.

By this stage you'll be well on the road to saying what you want to say the way you want to say it. You'll be able to speak more articulately.

But let's face it, no matter how brilliant your presentation, if nobody hears you, you've wasted a lot of preparation and delivery time.

Does your audience want to say, "Louder! Louder!"? Does your speech coach tell you, "Speak up!"? So you speak up, and then you find yourself shouting at the audience. Shouting has two negative consequences. It results in an irritating stridency and it can lead to a sore throat, hoarseness, laryngitis, and, in the extreme, nodes on the vocal cords. Frequently, these nodes must be surgically removed.

A BEAUTIFUL VOICE IS ESSENTIAL TO GOOD GROOMING

I'm sure you would agree that audibility is essential in all verbal communication. But do you realize the importance of a pleasant, beautiful voice? What an advantage it is! I maintain that a beautiful voice is the essential ingredient of not only persuasive communication but also good grooming. I believe a beautiful, resonant voice is more important to the sustained impression you make on people than expensive clothes, jewelry, and perfume.

Some people are self-conscious about having a foreign accent. Let me add one thing. There is nothing essentially wrong with having an accent if it's pleasant. If it sounds refined and warm, an accent, whether it's regional English, French, Italian, Russian, or Chinese, can be charming. In fact, it can be an advantage. It sets you apart from the common herd. However, if you sound coarse, you can and should do something about it. And it's easy. But not automatic.

Some years back I attended the opening night of a Broadway show. Afterward, with snow falling softly outside, we stood in the lobby with several other couples, making plans for apres-theater activity. One of the women was in her late thirties and extremely attractive. There were flowers in her seventy-five-dollar coiffeur. Her mink coat came down to her ankles. From her ears dangled diamond earrings. Stunning!

But when she opened her mouth to speak, out came a voice that sounded like a terrified, gaggling goose. This woman was well educated, but she sounded coarse. She sounded ignorant. She sounded vulgar. What a pity! The money she spent on her appearance would have been more advantageously spent on cultivating her voice.

Do you remember the sound created by rubbing your fingernails down a slate blackboard? Or the sensation created by eating spinach with sand in it? Too many voices have those same negative effects on audiences. Listeners don't realize that the quality of the speaker's voice has left them tense, irritable, and less able to remember main points.

YOU WERE BORN WITH A BEAUTIFUL VOICE

Listen to the pleasing voices of children. No matter how you sound now, you, too, started life with a beautiful voice. More than likely, you don't need speech therapy. A dedicated application of the method I've developed will help most of you get back to the voice nature gave you. At the same time, my method will help you project your voice to the back of even the largest room without strain and without needing a microphone, although there are times when you do need a mike—for instance, in a huge convention center.

My approach is two-pronged. First, I'll tell you how to exploit nature's way of learning how to speak. Second, I'll show you how to enrich and project your voice using breath-support and voice-placement techniques I developed as I trained executives all over the United States and Europe.

It is, essentially, a matter of the right management of the voice to express the various emotions—of speaking loudly, softly, or between the two; of high, low, or intermediate pitch; of the various rhythms that suit various subjects. These are the three things—volume of sound, modulation of pitch, and rhythm-that a speaker bears in mind.
—Aristotle, *Rhetoric*

EXPLOIT NATURE'S WAY OF LEARNING GOOD PRONUNCIATION

When you watch television news broadcasts, you probably notice the disparity between the language spoken by the newscaster and the man in the street. They may come from the same region. They may even have had an equal academic education. But they don't speak the same way. Like Professor Higgins in *My Fair Lady*, I wonder, "Why can't the English teach the English how to speak?" Why can't America educate its youth to speak the language correctly? By the way, this lack of emphasis on good pronunciation is true whether you're from France, Germany, Sweden, Spain, or China.

At the Theatre Academy of Long Island, many of the teenagers didn't think pronunciation was important. They spoke with a New York, "Brooklynese" accent. When in class, they spoke perfect English, as they had been taught, but among their friends they reverted to "New Yorkese." So they were instructed to perform the following experiment. They went to a local department store and tried to get service speaking vernacular "New Yorkese" and then reported back. Universally, they said they were pushed around, overlooked, and snubbed. They got no respect. Then they returned to the store speaking standard, American, nonphony broadcast English. The difference was as night to day. They said they'd been waited on with respect.

Most of my students had little trouble getting into good colleges because they spoke so beautifully.

I mentioned standard, American, nonphony broadcast English. No matter where you hear a newscast, you hear the language spoken perfectly. Voice quality and pronunciation are as near perfection as you can get. That's because, in order to get their jobs, newscasters have had to reeducate themselves to pronounce standard, broadcast English.

Preferred English pronunciation was arbitrarily agreed upon somewhere about the time of the First World War when speech teachers from all English-speaking countries gathered in a convention and decided that this way of pronouncing a word sounded better than that way. They wisely made allowances for some regional usage, and that's why there are often several correct ways of pronouncing a word. But the criterion remains—what sounds best?

The thrust of the first prong—exploiting nature's way of learning—is to learn how to pronounce words the best way. To accomplish this on your own, listen to newscasters. Pay particular attention to how they pronounce the words. Listen to the modulation of their voices. Imitate.

If you're not clear about what modulation is, picture this. When you turn up a radio to full volume, the sound blares. It distorts. It's harsh. It rattles. It's abrasive. It's strident. When you turn the volume down slightly, the music is suddenly pleasurable.

Your voice works the same way. Turn the volume down and your voice is more pleasant. You hear the music. You hear the notes. So bellowing at the audience is wrong because it usually results in an unpleasant reaction. When you learn to place your voice correctly, your voice will sound pleasant.

A symphony orchestra has over a hundred instruments. You might think the sound would blast, but it doesn't. They don't play too loudly because they modulate the sounds of their instruments to create the effect the composer and conductor want.

Whenever you turn on the television, newscasters provide free pronunciation lessons for you, so you can use Mother Nature's own way of learning. Why do French children speak French? German children German? Chinese children Chinese? Why do northeasterners sound different from westerners and southerners? They didn't learn in any school; they learned at home by listening to the people around them.

Thus, you must use listening as nature's way to reeducate yourself to pronounce words correctly.

I try to be very careful of the final consonants D, T, P, and so forth, so that the ends of my words may be clearly heard and understood.
—Sir John Gielgud, quoted in *Actors Talk about Acting*

Exercise

Listen to the way your favorite newscaster pronounces the words. Pretend you're a newscaster. (Not to develop the ability to coordinate words with thoughts, as you did in Chapter 3, but to learn to pronounce.) Using a tape recorder, read from a newspaper or news magazine. Try to pronounce words the way the newscaster does.

Take your time. For this purpose, you don't have to talk as rapidly as he or she does.

Listen to yourself on tape; then read again, correcting your pronunciation.

In a surprisingly short time your speech will begin to

improve. You will begin to speak standard, unphoney American English, or English English, or French, or Japanese. (The author hopes this book will sell in countries other than the United States.)

LEARN THE TWO ELEMENTS OF VOICE BEAUTY

The second prong in the development of a strong, rich voice that projects depends on two factors—breath support and voice placement.

Enrich Your Voice with Breath Support

Too many times, lack of breath support produces a weak voice. For good projection, you must start with your lungs full of air. Always start speaking by taking a nice, leisurely deep breath. Fill your lungs with air. Do it now. Do not strain. It must feel comfortable. If you feel any sort of a strain, it's wrong. Then at every pause (usually marked at a comma or semicolon), take a little catchbreath to replenish your supply of air. At the end of the sentence, take a full breath.

You'll achieve two desirable results. Your voice won't peter out before you reach the end of the sentence, and you won't lose the last few words of each sentence. And with your pauses, you'll give the audience a chance to digest your last bit of wisdom. Too many speakers talk in run-on paragraphs, sometimes in run-on pages.

Exercise

Find something to read aloud from—a newspaper, novel, or speech. The *New York Times* prints most important speeches verbatim. Mark the script for each catch breaeth (brief pause) and each full breath (full pause). Use a slash mark (**/**) for a brief pause. Use an X mark (**X**) for a full stop at the end of a thought. See how this method works using Lincoln's Gettysburg Address:

Four score and seven years ago/our fathers brought forth

on this continent/a new nation,/conceived in Liberty,/and dedicated to the proposition that all men are created equal.χ

Now we are engaged in a great civil war,/testing whether that nation/or any nation/so conceived and so dedicated,/can long endure/We are met on a great battlefield of that war.χ We have come to dedicate a portion of that field/as a final resting-place/for those/who here gave their lives/that that nation might live/It is altogether fitting and proper/that we should do this, etc. χ

Read your selection aloud into your recorder; take a catch breath at the slash mark and a full breath at the X mark. This method is based on how broadcast voice-over announcers mark their scripts for exact interpretation. Because time means money, they have a minimal time for rehearsal.

Listen to yourself on tape. Repeat the exercise over and over again. This repetition will give you three benefits:

- You'll develop a stronger, sustained voice.
- You'll eliminate voice strain.
- You'll achieve a more natural reading style.

Next, a brief word about diaphragmatic breathing. You may have heard that singers and actors "breathe from the diaphragm." The diaphragm is the layer of muscle situated at the base of your rib cage.

Of course, this method of breathing is the recommended one because you have the greatest lung capacity near the diaphragm. However, you shouldn't attempt learning to breathe from the diaphragm by yourself. It can be confusing because it's hard to understand. You should have the personal supervision of a qualified speech therapist or speech or singing teacher to guide you. If you follow my recommendations above, you will have sufficient breath support for most of your needs.

Project Your Voice with Voice Placement

Your voice will do what you tell it to do. In a way, it's like a computer: you give it commands and it obeys. When you want to sing "Yankee Doodle," you don't get "In the Good

During the twenties, one of the most beloved men of New York's literary and newspaper crowd was a warm-hearted minor actor and singer named Ed MacNamara. At one time, the unambitious MacNamara was seized by the feeling that he should develop his vocal talents. The ambition subsided, but not before he had managed an informal coaching session with Enrico Caruso. Forever after, he told of the great tenor's simple recipe for successful singing: "Mac, you know whatta you do when you shit? Singing—it's the same thing, only up!"

—The Little, Brown Book of Anecdotes, edited by Clifton Fadiman

Old Summer Time.'' When you tell it to go soft, it goes soft. When you tell it to go loud, it goes loud. Speaking loudly without hurting yourself is why proper voice placement becomes so essential to your development as a professional speaker.

The big secret of proper placement is voice focus. Most books on voice placement make placement a big, big deal. When I was an acting student, it was only after about three months of daily speech classes that I finally caught on. At my Theatre Academy of Long Island I was able to teach placement in about five sessions. But when I began to give executive workshops in two days, with only an hour and a half of that time to address the problem, I had to develop a new method. I've been using it for some eighteen years and it works, as thousands of business executives can attest.

I'm telling you all this because at first blush what I'm recommending may seem a little complicated. It isn't. It's probably one of the simplest methods ever devised. To some of you the instructions may even sound silly. They aren't. They work. Just follow the instructions one step at a time.

Before we begin, let's first explore how a poor speaking voice is created. Then I'll show you how to create a beautiful speaking voice.

Let me introduce you to Brunhilde McGillicudy, my speech assistant. She'll help me explain voice placement.

With both good and poor speakers, the voice is initiated by a column of air from the lungs (A) causing the vocal cords (B), a V-shaped band of muscle situated in the larynx, to vibrate, creating sound. This sound then proceeds to the mouth cavity (C), where, with the help of lips, tongue, and teeth, it forms the vowels and consonants that become words. From the mouth, these words are directed at the audience.

The trouble is that too many people use only their mouths to project with and therefore render themselves inaudible to anyone beyond the first row.

''So,'' you ask, ''isn't the voice supposed to come out of the mouth?''

Yes. The voice is indeed supposed to come out of the mouth. But when you are using *only* the mouth as a resonating chamber, you are using less than half of your voice poten-

I think that Stanislavsky was probably the first to admit that voice projection was necessary . . . Nothing is more maddening to the public than to pay to see an actor and not hear him or see him properly all the evening, however much he may have integrity in his performance and however much his shoulder blades may express his feelings.
—Sir John Gielgud, quoted in *Actors Talk about Acting*

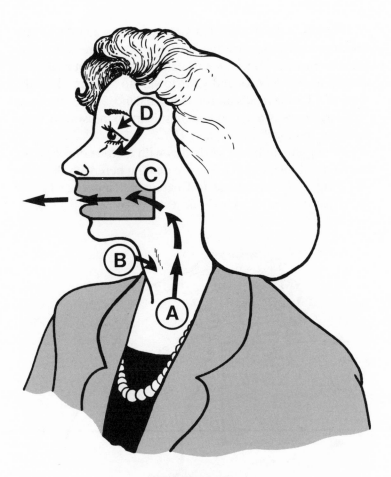

BRUNHILDE

tial. That's how too many people speak. These people are the mumblers, the inaudible, the mousey-sounding. By using the mouth cavity only, you must use your throat muscles to achieve more volume. It is the use of those muscles that causes the stridency, the sore throat, or worse.

You see, when you talk "lungs, windpipe, and out the mouth," you are talking monaurally. And everyone in the world is born with a stereo system. The primary amplification and resonating mode in your scull is located above and below your eyes in the sinus passages (D). Sinuses are hollow bones that act as highfidelity baffles in that they take a thin sound, reverberate it, enrich it, and enlarge it.

Through the use of both sinus passages and the mouth cavity you will acquire the full potential of the voice you were born with. Professionals call the area in your face between your eyebrows and your lower lip "the mask of the face." To achieve a beautiful, fully-balanced voice that projects and is easily audible, you must learn to thrust your voice through the mask of the face (E).

I'm going to help you do this with a little concentration and a lot of imagination. We are dealing here with the mental imagery I recommend in Chapter 8. That imagery will help you remember what's necessary forever.

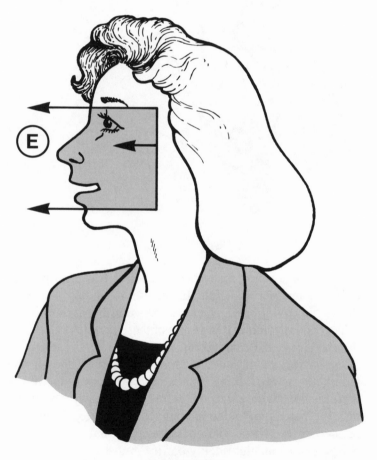

BRUNHILDE

The idea is to get your voice out of your throat and into the mask. Here's how you do it. Look at the next illustration of Brunhilde. You must imagine you have a hole in the top of your head about an inch in diameter. Projecting from that hole is a tube about ten inches long (F). Now you are ready to begin.

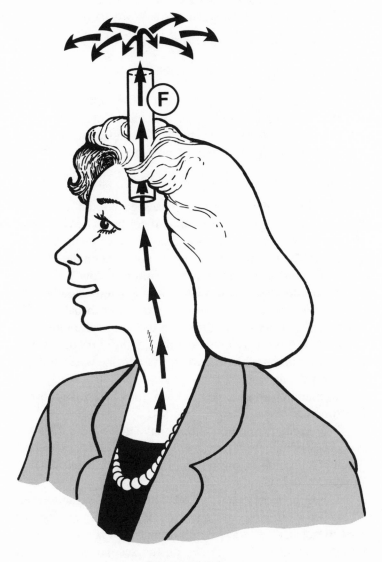

BRUNHILDE

Exercise 1

As a practice selection, use either of the following.
SELECTION 1

> The Moving Finger writes, and, having writ,
> Moves on, nor all your Piety nor Wit
> Shall lure it back to cancel half a Line,
> Nor all your Tears wash out a Word of it.
>
> —Edward FitzGerald, *The Rubaiyat of Omar Khayyam*

SELECTION 2

> Heard melodies are sweet, but those unheard
> Are sweeter; therefore, ye soft pipes, play on;
> Not to the sensual ear, but, more endear'd,
> Pipe to the spirit ditties of no tone:
>
> —John Keats, "Ode on a Grecian Urn"

To begin, recite whichever passage you choose twice in quick succession into your tape recorder. The first time, start with a nice easy breath, and say it the way you normally would. The second time, keeping your eye on the illustration of Brunhilde, pretend that you aren't sending your voice out of your mouth as you recite (although you actually are), but that you are sending it straight from your throat, up past your nose and eyes, and thrusting it through the tube. Try to make each word ricochet off the ceiling. Of course, this is physically impossible, but when you imagine yourself doing this, you do the job.

Remember at all times to keep your breath support as illustrated above. Listen to yourself.

The second time you should have achieved a 15 to 75 percent enrichment of your voice. If you have a nasal twang, placing the voice in the mask of the face will eliminate it in short order.

Caution! Don't strain. And don't be an eager beaver. These are exercises, and any exercise that's overdone can lead to negative effects. Begin doing this exercise for five minutes, then do ten minutes on the second day. Twenty minutes a day should be sufficient.

Exercise 2

The following voice-production exercise regimen has been used successfully by my pupils for over twenty years. It works best when you're sitting in a straight chair.

1. *Head Roll*
   Drop your chin onto your chest. Roll your head slowly toward your right shoulder, back, left shoulder, and front (five times). Repeat to the left (five times).

2. *"Blah-Blah"*
   Still sitting, let your chin fall onto your chest. Stick your tongue onto your lower lip. Close your eyes. Say "blah-blah" for a count of 10. Take a breath. Do it again. (Repeat five times or more.)

3. *Yawn*
   Do nice, long, leisurely yawns (five times or more).

4. *"Hum"*
   With your lips barely touching, hum for a slow count of 5. Take a breath and repeat (five times or more).

5. *"Ma-May-Me-Moe-Moo"*
   Do the same as in item 4.

6. *"Whisper"*
   Choose either Selection 1 or 2 or the following children's rhyme. Whisper it once or twice.

   > Mary had a little lamb,
   > Its fleece was white as snow;
   > And everywhere that Mary went,
   > The lamb was sure to go.
   > It followed her to school one day,
   > Which was against the rule;
   > It made the children laugh and play,
   > To see a lamb in school.

The nice thing about these voice exercises is that you don't have to carve out a special time in your busy schedule to do them. You can practice while taking a shower, driving the car, mowing the lawn, cooking, or washing dishes. We don't recommend practicing while shaving, however.

Practicing these exercises will take care of voice quality. You will achieve the full potential of your voice. Most people are born with a symphony orchestra of a voice but go through life using a five-piece combo. Your voice will become balanced. Retaining the symphony analogy, if your voice is gutteral and throaty, you'll gain violins. If your voice is strident, highpitched, and thin, you'll gain body—cellos and baritone horns.

PROJECT WITHOUT STRAIN

The above exercises will also give you additional projection. Even that projection, however, might not be sufficient. I must point out at this juncture that I do not advocate a continuous avalanche of bombastic sound. At all times, you need to sound as if you are speaking conversationally. Use the normal speech dynamics of speaking with natural expression as if you are talking to your closest friend. This method, used by actors, will project even a whisper to the back of the room. Notice how singers can sing very, very softly (pianissimo) and still be heard in the third balcony. Hamlet's "To be or not to be" speech can be delivered with hardly any voice at all, yet heard distinctly in the last row.

As I've said before, it's dangerous to use the throat muscles to thrust your voice forward. Trained actors or opera singers perform for two or three hours and don't injure themselves. In my workshops I usually talk about seven hours a day for two days twice a week in large rooms, sometimes with bad acoustics. I'm easily heard in the last row, and I never become hoarse or lose my voice.

Here's how to achieve safe projection. Once more, I'm going to ask you to use your imagination. Think in terms of wind velocity. The larger the room, the more velocity you need. If you feel strain in your larynx area, you're not doing it correctly.

- Intimate conversation (basic)—5 m.p.h. velocity
- Dinner table, party—10 m.p.h. velocity (stiff breeze)
- Medium-sized room—30 m.p.h. velocity (gale)
- Very large room, small auditorium, theatre—75 m.p.h. velocity (hurricane)
- Gymnasium, large auditorium, outdoors—100 m.p.h. velocity (tornado)

If you're going to speak for more than five minutes in the last situation, I recommend a microphone.

DON'T BACKSLIDE

A word of warning! Let me paraphrase Iago in *Othello*: "Beware, my Lord, of peer pressure."

As a result of this book, you're going to look better and you're going to sound better. To achieve these improvements beautifully in your room, study, or classroom is not enough. You're going to have to bring the improvements into your office, conference room, and home. You might be afraid that your spouse, your child, or a co-worker or friend will notice the change and think negatively of you. You might imagine such a person saying, "You're putting on airs" or "You're getting too fancy for me!" And you might be tempted to lapse back into your old, bad habits.

They'll notice the change, all right, but they will admire your desire to improve, and they'll rush right out and buy a copy of this book.

The way you flaunt your weight loss after dieting, your new car, your new hairdo, or your new golf clubs is the way you must flaunt your new professionalism. In a few days they'll forget you ever did things differently.

I once was a producer at one of the largest film production companies in New York City. Every Monday morning a staff meeting was conducted by the head of the company. He was almost totally bald. For years we faced him across his desk. Then one Monday he arrived with a full head of

You must always be like a jockey on a race horse—watching, watchful, watch it—listening all the time to one's self. I mean, jockeys don't ever dare let the horse stretch its neck out, do they? They've had it then. I don't care how big the acting is, how loud you're roaring, how stridently you're screaming—it must never be absolutely quite at the top of your voice. If you hit the ceiling, then the audience can suddenly see the measure of you. Suddenly you look weak instead of strong—and they think, "Oh my, he is straining himself, isn't he?"
—Sir Laurence Olivier, quoted in *Famous Actors and Actresses on the American Stage*

hair. Within the week it was hard to remember that he had once been bald.

To summarize: cultivate your voice. Don't neglect this most important part of your grooming. Use nature's way of learning—imitate the pronunciation of newscasters and others whose speech you admire. Enrich your voice by developing proper breath support and voice placement. You won't ever hear anyone asking you to speak louder again. And I'm betting you'll get all sorts of compliments on your beautiful voice.

5

HOW TO PRACTICE PERFORMANCE SKILLS

What you know is important, but the difference between a speaker who keeps the audience awake or asleep is the packaging of that knowledge. And that entails using storytelling to practice performance skills just as the golfer uses a bucket of balls.

The best thing I can do for you, the reader of this book, is to tell you not to read this book at all, but to put you into a musical comedy, like *Auntie Mame, South Pacific,* or *The King and I*, rehearse you ten or twelve weeks, and then send you out on the road to play the musical in twenty different cities.

What you would learn is beyond value. You'd get the feel of an audience. You'd know where to stand. You'd know how not to talk too fast. You'd know how to take a skeptical audience and get them enthusiastic. You'd be able to wake up a bored audience. You'd have excellent timing and know how to use dramatic pauses.

Unfortunately, you would run into cost accounting because, if you're like most people, you can't devote six months of your valuable earning power to do this. The closest I can get to putting you into a rehearsed production is for you to learn what people like Bill Cosby, Dick Van Dyke, Bob Hope, Carol Burnett, Red Buttons, Frank Sinatra, and Woody Allen know.

TELL A STORY

It isn't a mere coincidence that these actors started performing as stand-up comedians, entertainers, and singers. Night after night of getting audience approval and appreciation in competition with table talk, food, and strong drink honed their acting skills to a fine finish. Stanislavsky used to have his actors entertain in cabarets to improve their timing. I've been using the medium of storytelling to instill and strengthen performance skills in people who need to speak for a living in classrooms, conference rooms, assembly halls, and churches.

My telling you what is needed is not enough. It's only the beginning. As I said in Chapter 3, speaking effectively is physical. You cannot learn a physical skill merely by understanding what's needed. You must have a means to practice that skill.

You can't go to your Aunt Agatha's party and say to her guests, ''Hey folks, let me interrupt these festivities for

> *The Stanislavsky method is intended, I believe—and if I'm wrong I use it this way, nevertheless—I think it is intended to be used as a method of preparation for work, not as a method employable in the instance of work . . . Which means that instead of employing the Stanislavsky method for two hours a night in a theatre, I employ it for two or three months in the preparation of that work, so that when I go on the stage, or in front of a camera, my function becomes organic and instant and natural, spontaneous and full, because I have a frame of reference for every want, every need, every desire that is registered on my emotion boards.*
> —Sidney Poitier, quoted in *Actors Talk about Acting*

> *You may not be inspired or feel a feeling, but you should always be able to go out there and tell a simple, clear story.*
> —John Strasberg, quoted in *The New Generation of Acting Teachers*

a moment. Uncle Charlie, put down that canape. Cousin Elsie, you can get back to that glass of punch in an hour. I need to rehearse the presentation I'm going to make next Tuesday.'' You know what will happen: they'll throw you out the window.

But if you say, ''Hey, I heard this great story about a donkey and a lazy camel,'' they'll be all ears. And you'll be practicing performance skills where it does the most good: in front of an audience. (You *should* rehearse the actual presentation. We'll show you how in Chapter 9.)

Humorous stories are your medium of perfecting performance skills. Incidentally, it's the medium used by most actors to sustain their techniques.

Actors spend most of their time being unemployed. The membership of Actors' Equity is 85 percent chronically unemployed. The income of the average actor is less than $10,000. And that's with superstars like Paul Newman, Sylvester Stallone, Meryl Streep, and Dustin Hoffman making a million dollars on one end and the rest of the acting community on the other.

The actor, unlike other kinds of artists, must have an audience to consummate the marriage. A musician can sing or play an instrument, or a painter can paint, but the actor must have an audience.

Audiences exist all over. So the artist, the actor artist, uses storytelling to practice techniques just as the golfer uses a bucket of balls. Storytelling is the actor's driving range. If you ever go to a party where there are actors, they're telling stories. If you travel with actors, on the road, on the train, on the plane, they're swapping stories. You know what happens backstage in the green room? They're telling stories. They practice their German or Irish dialects. They practice their timing. They practice their entrances. They hone their acting talents through telling stories. (Appendix A contains stories for you to practice.)

Incidentally, when I talk about telling stories, I don't mean cracking one-liners, nor do I mean that cracking one-liners or jokes is part of a presenter's job. I use telling stories as a medium for practice. If a person wants to tell a story to make a point, okay, but to come loaded with one-liners

A good raconteur at the dinner table or in the drawing room has just as much sense of timing as the actor. The actor's timing must be adjusted to other actors and to an audience. Perhaps that may be technique, though even it is largely ear training. But the moment timing becomes methodical, deliberate and over-studied—simply an exercise in technique—the actor becomes like a clock ticking. And precision is bad. It is far better for the actor to be a little off beat, to jangle!

—Lynn Fontanne, quoted in Famous Actors and Actresses on the American Stage

The real power is the power of being potent, feeling I am communicating these words and emotions to another human being.

—Zoe Caldwell, quoted in Actress to Actress

is inappropriate most of the time. If a person is naturally witty, or if wittiness is appropriate, wit will add spice to the proceedings. However, a person without a natural wit trying to be funny can be deadly.

The more you perform, the better a speaker you'll become. Performing perfects your techniques. It perfects your skills. It perfects your packaging.

PACKAGE YOUR MESSAGE

Packaging your message is important. Yes, I said packaging. I spent many years producing TV commercials for advertising agencies, and I learned a lot about the customer's business. One of the most valuable lessons was how important the packaging of a product is in merchandising it.

Reprinted with permission of Creators Syndicate, Inc.

Very often, the cost of the package will be greater than the product. I have a friend who once worked as a perfume chemist. He told me that a leading brand of perfume cost less than a dollar to produce but that the bottle and the box cost three or four times that.

In your case, the product you purvey is your expertise. The package is you.

Several years ago, researchers found that what a person sees has eight times the impact of what he or she hears. When a speaker is addressing an audience, 7 percent of the impact is what the audience hears, and 38 percent is voice quality. Is your voice strident or abrasive? Do you sound educated? The rest is what the audience sees, how the speaker looks.

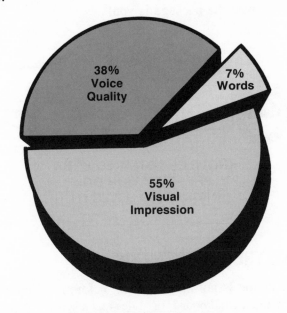

PRESENTATION IMPACT

So the content of a speech amounts to only 7 percent of the impact made on an audience. This is why we have slept so successfully through many a lecture by eminent professors, doctors, and advisors to presidents. Being smart is only the beginning.

Don't be too discouraged by this fact. Say 7 percent of the car in the following illustration is the motor; this represents what you know. The remaining 93 percent is the chrome, the shape, the upholstery, and the color. Without the 7 percent—the motor—the car is not going to move. If you don't know what you're talking about, the audience will catch up with you.

How many people buy the car for the motor? Few. Most

of the time they buy the packaging, right? They buy the ego. They buy the prestige. An old advertising slogan says, "Don't sell the steak, sell the sizzle."

What you know is important, but the difference between a speaker who keeps an audience awake or asleep is the packaging of that knowledge. And that entails performance skills. Because the package is you!

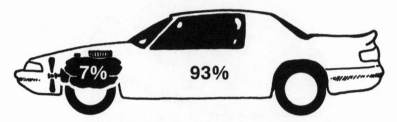

**KNOWLEDGE MAKES YOUR
PRESENTATION GO;
PACKAGING SELLS IT!**

DEFINE THE PRESENTATION

A presentation is not only standing before a group with a flipchart and a chalkboard, or slides and a screen. A presentation is any time you have to motivate another person, whatever the purpose. It could be across a desk in your office, across a coffee table at a cocktail party, or on the telephone where the other person can't even see you.

If you want to motivate a person to come dance with you, that takes performance skills.

To keep it simple, I'm going to refer to stand-up presentation skills, because most people are pretty good sitting down and presenting. The problem always arises in a standing position, because most people—like you—equate a presentation with a trip to the dentist. It's going to be a painfully excruciating experience. But it's got to be done. You've got to go to the dentist. You've got to make the presentation.

What is the usual attitude?

"Let's get this darn thing over with as quickly and painlessly as possible."

CHECK YOUR ATTITUDE

Put yourself in the audience for a moment. What do you see?

You see an accomplished person . . . let me pause here after the word *accomplished*. You know, they don't ask a dummy to make a presentation. They don't say, "You know David Gardner? He knows nothing; he's a nerd. Let's have him make a presentation." They don't do that. If they ask you to teach the class, to visit the customer, to explain a product, they think you've got some thing on the ball. So back to my original sentence . . .

You see an accomplished person get up before an audience something like this: he or she shuffles to the front of the room and stands there in a slumped position, with cold perspiration, wet, clammy hands, and gelatinous knees gently knocking. And that person will remain in sort of an individual isolation booth and deliver to the carpet a three-hour presentation in twenty minutes flat.

Do you recognize this person?

That's the one who put you to sleep that time. This poor soul, sweating, trembling, and talking to the carpet, is in the grips of humankind's number one fear, public speaking. Commonly known as stage fright.

I feel sorry for that poor soul, because he or she is going through needless and mostly self-imposed agony. Do you know who that person is terrified of?

That person is terrified of . . . *you!*

Now, did you ever meet a nicer person than yourself? You are open-minded, compassionate, intelligent, understanding, knowledgeable, charitable, and insightful. You, dear friend, happen to be a typical audience member. If you were speaking to you, would you be afraid of yourself? Of course not!

CONSIDER THE AUDIENCE A FRIEND

Let me tell you about audiences. I've been appearing before audiences of one kind or another since I was eight years old. I've never met an audience that was out to get me. I've always

There's an energy that goes from the stage to the audience and is sent back to the stage. Theatre is not a spectator sport. Something should happen . . . You create something for the audience which is specific to them.

—Glenda Jackson, quoted in Clare Calvin, "As You Like It Or Not," *Drama*, 1986.

found audiences courteous, tolerant, and supportive—both theatrical and business audiences.

As I said in a previous chapter, if you forget a word or an acronym, people will furnish it. Several years ago the newspapers ran a story about Richard Harris, the renowned British actor who has spent many years starring in the long, successful run of the musical *Camelot*. He was playing in London's West End to a very sophisticated audience. At that time, he had played the role about 500 times. Halfway through the song "What Do the Simple Folk Do?" he went blank; he couldn't remember the next line of the lyrics to save his life.

Out of character, he walked out on the apron of the stage (that's the place in front of the curtain) and explained that he could not remember the next line. There was laughter, sympathetic laughter. No booing, no hissing, and no one asking for money back. Then the whole West End audience stood up and gave him a standing ovation for about fifteen minutes.

"Sure," you're saying to yourself, "that was a theater audience, and that was a star with a track record. How would a business audience react to such a circumstance?"

One of my clients is the Governor's Office of Employee Relations of the State of New York, one of whose functions is the welfare and upgrading of professional skills of its management-level civil servants. I had just related the above anecdote about Richard Harris when a very dignified man in his forties who looked like a bank president stood up and told about his experience with an audience that could be counted on in a crunch.

He said that he was a civil engineer, and part of his job had to do with construction and maintenance of every bridge in the state—thousands of bridges. His specialty was metal stress. As an expert, he was invited to make a presentation to an international convention of civil engineers at the University of Wisconsin. He came loaded with charts, slides, and statistics. He got up to speak in front of this august assemblage and went completely blank. He was so petrified that he couldn't remember his own name. Not only that, he thought he was going to faint.

He explained that if he were to faint, it would have been

tragic for him. He had a license to pilot a plane, and if he ever fainted, his license would be taken away. Well, these engineers from all over the world nursed him through the beginning of his presentation. They changed slides and they furnished acronyms until he regained his composure.

This is just one of many similar stories I hear at most sessions I teach. Give people half a chance and they behave in a very humane way.

Once I was to conduct a workshop for a new client, one of the top ten advertising agencies. For the occasion I went out and bought a brand new suit. About ten minutes before I was to start, I took Winston Churchill's advice and went to the men's room. In readjusting my clothing, I discovered that the zipper had broken. I couldn't zip it up. My home was an hour away, and, besides, twelve account executives were waiting for me in the conference room.

I bit the bullet. I went in, greeted my class, and explained the situation. Oh, there was laughter, but it wasn't directed at me. One of the women reached into her purse and handed me a large safety pin. I left the room for a moment, made the necessary adjustment, and proceeded. That group turned out to be one of the most congenial I ever worked with.

Sometimes people are helpful even in an adversary situation. Several years ago there was a strike of actors belonging to the Screen Actors' Guild. It was a bitter fight and was front-page news while it lasted. At one of the negotiating sessions, with management on one side of the table going at it hot and heavy with union representatives on the other side of the table, a member of the management team got something caught in his throat and couldn't get a word out. The head of the union delegation handed him a glass of water and said in a friendly way, "Here. Drink this." Then they went back to fighting.

The reaction of the audience is an integral part of any performance.
—Charles Laughton, quoted in
Backstage with Actors

[The Method] is to be as true and real, and alive and fresh in the part each time. That's your job.
—Maureen Stapleton, quoted in
Actors Talk about Acting

LEARN WHAT AN AUDIENCE WILL NOT TOLERATE

There are things an audience will not tolerate. Phoniness is the biggest no-no. You know how it is when someone is trying to act like a big shot and you know damn well they're not. Or they are trying to act humble and you know damn well they're not. Phoniness glares at you.

This is why the best thing you can do for yourself is to be yourself. The best style is to be yourself. Whatever that is.

When asked "What do you think about onstage in The Iceman Cometh?" Barnard Hughes replied, "I must admit that I ran over a couple of shopping lists this week. Generally I've found that you'd better stay with the play; if you drift out of it, you begin to hear the zzzzs all over the place."

Barnard Hughes, quoted in
Caught in the Act:
New York Actors Face to Face

Audiences will not tolerate boredom. And they will not tolerate it if you don't know what you're talking about, if you come up there and try to really bull them.

In all three instances, they will not leave. They won't throw rocks at you. They *will* take defensive action. Most people hate to go to meetings because they anticipate the excruciating boredom. So, if you prove them right, they'll retreat into their own self-concerns and clang shut their gates of privacy. Their eyes will be open but glazed over. You'll be expounding on cash flow and they'll be thinking "Shall I have hamburgers or lamb chops for dinner?" Or "Shall I go to the movies or do my income tax?" Or "How can I get out of having dinner with the Harrises?"

The way to keep those gates of privacy open is to know what you're talking about, to be yourself, and to package yourself using skillful performance techniques.

The person in the isolation booth talking to the carpet a mile a minute is wrong.

What's the right way?

What are these performance skills that I have been touting? I'll show you in Chapters 6, 7, and 8.

PART THREE

DELIVERING A WINNING PRESENTATION

6

HOW TO DEVELOP A NATURAL PLATFORM STYLE

Use your best skills un-pretentiously, do your homework, and commit yourself to a positive objective. Then you'll achieve a natural, self-confident delivery style that lets you talk with your audience, not at them.

The best style is to be natural. To be yourself. Developing the natural in yourself starts with your attitude going in—your attitude when you begin to prepare your presentation.

How do you begin to develop your attitude?

DEFINE YOUR OBJECTIVE

The answer is basic, almost corny. But if you think about it, the world is constructed on a solid foundation of corn. What we call corn is a truism beaten to death. So let's cut the corn and go back to the truism.

Why do you make a presentation anyway?

First, either you have something to sell or you want to inspire. The purpose underlying many presentations is the desire to motivate somebody to

- Buy a product or service
- Join the softball team
- Contribute to a charity
- Join the navy
- Solicit funds
- Hire you
- Promote you
- Marry you
- Reduce expenses
- Stop sinning

Second, you may use the presentation to educate and to inform:

- This is how it works.
- This is why it's better.
- This is what my department does.
- This is what my colleagues did with the money.

You start, therefore, by clearly defining your purpose or, in other words, by defining your objective.

Your objective must never be "to deliver a presentation" or "to make a speech." Your objective must be what

I had a line in Quadrille in London that I thought was amusing. I was playing this American railroad man and I had to say, "Well, perhaps after all I will have a cup of tea," and actually, you know, he should have had a shot of bourbon. To me it was amusing. It did for a little while get a sort of smile . . . but then I lost it. And I said to Lynn, "Why have I lost that laugh?" "Because," she said, "You are asking for a laugh."

—Alfred Lunt, quoted in
Actors Talk about Acting

It has been called objective, action, or intention. Some people don't call it anything . . . I myself don't care if you call it spinach, . . . if you do it, because it is one of the most important elements in acting. [Substitute the word speaking for acting.]

—Robert Lewis,
Method or Madness

you want to accomplish with that presentation or speech. One of the first things an actor learns to ask is "What do I want to accomplish? Not *how* I say the line, but *why* I say the line."

State the objective positively.

"Very often people set negative goals," writes Dr. Steven Danish, Professor of Human Development at Pennsylvania State University. "For example, 'I don't want to be nervous when I participate.' When you focus on a negative goal like not being nervous, what you eventually do is focus on your nervousness . . . In other words, setting a negative goal almost always ensures a negative outcome."

Saying "I mustn't forget," or "I mustn't laugh," or "I mustn't blush" means that you probably will forget, or laugh, or blush.

COMMIT YOURSELF

Committing yourself to a positive objective will help you to channel your thinking and to organize and write your presentation without too much wheel-spinning. Moreover, it will help you toward achieving a natural, self-confident style of delivery, which is important.

"Commit yourself" is two words. We've talked about the "commit" part. Now I'd like to add a word about "yourself."

You are the best thing you can give your audience.

Do you remember Walt Disney's Dumbo? Here was this elephant with huge ears and the ability to fly, but he was afraid until the cricket gave him a feather to hold. He didn't need the feather. In the sequence where he loses it, he finds out he can fly without it. Just like Dumbo didn't need the feather, you don't need the podium, the pointer, or the clipboard. They are tools, not crutches.

A little while ago, I was conducting a workshop for a prestigious corporation in Houston, Texas. During the lunch break I was fortunate enough to sit across the table from a very accomplished young woman. She was personable and well groomed, but, uncharacteristically for this company, very heavily albeit skillfully made up. This young woman

Concentration. That's it [the single most important element in acting]. It's so bloody difficult . . . I used to play a game at parties asking for a telegram that you most wanted to get. I remember one guest said, Am sending down gift of concentration. Signed, God. True. True.
—Constance Cummings, quoted in *Actress to Actress*

Trust. Part of acting is having the security to turn yourself loose and let yourself go . . . Audiences believe what you believe. It's a matter of believing yourself. If I believe me, then you've got no choice. None at all.
—Morgan Freeman, quoted in *Caught in the Act: New York Actors Face to Face*

didn't need cosmetics to make her good-looking. (One of the skills I acquired as a casting director hiring models is the ability to burrow beneath the makeup job to see what's there.) She only needed a clean, washed face with perhaps a touch of lipstick. It saddened me, because that heavy application was this young woman's crutch. She didn't feel secure on her own.

Not all of us can be born with perfect features, but every last one of us can be beautiful. It's a matter of self-image.

I remember as a kid seeing films starring Elizabeth Bergner, a really fine actress. Naturally, she played the love interest, a femme fatale. In film after film she drove men mad with her beauty. She wasn't all that beautiful; to my candid child eyes she appeared only mildly pretty. But the audience as a whole was convinced that she was indeed a raving beauty. Why? Because she perceived herself as a raving beauty and therefore projected that quality.

Conceive of yourself as an authority committed to your subject. Do your homework, be yourself, and you will project authority. Many an actor, convincing you that he's a king, was washing dishes in some greasy-spoon restaurant two weeks ago.

> *[The keynote of my acting] is the ability to be caught up in a story, to really believe in a situation. That's the power of belief.*
>
> —Julie Harris, quoted in *Actress to Actress*

LEARN THE WHY AND HOW OF PLATFORM STYLE

Let's examine style in presentation. Suppose you go to buy a new car. In one showroom you meet a salesperson who seems to be interested only in earning a fast commission. He reels off the features of various models in a mechanical way and cites prices with undertones that reflect his opinion of what you can or cannot afford. He gives you the impression that he's doing you a favor just talking to you.

Then there is the salesperson who greets you warmly, treats you like an old friend, listens to your needs, points out the differences between one model and another, and shows a genuine interest in helping you decide. You might very well buy from a person like this, and not only that, you might just seek her out the next time you're in the market for a new car.

Both of these people made a presentation based on the same facts. Which presentation would you prefer? Which kind of presenter do you want to be?

CONSIDER YOURSELF A TEACHER

A good way to begin to develop a natural style is to consider yourself not a pitchman but a teacher. You know something the audience doesn't . . . and you tell the audience what you know. That's teaching. The teaching element of every presentation should be very strong, even if the audience consists of colleagues, some of whom may have much more prestigious titles than you do. You, the presenter, should understand that during the presentation you outrank anyone in the audience. You are the authority. You are the teacher.

Taking on the role of a teacher does something very positive for your delivery. You'll find that you will not talk too fast. People primarily concerned with not forgetting their facts and figures have a tendency to race through their presentation lickety-split. The attitude "I am teaching" gives you a more personalized feeling. You communicate more intimately with your audience. You are more apt to look at them and therefore derive the benefit of instant feedback even though that input is usually nonverbal in the form of smiles, nods, and doubtful looks.

There's no play there until the audience is in their seats. You can't perform a play to an empty house. You need that audience to throw those vibrations back.
—Shelley Winters, quoted in *Actress to Actress*

PLAY OFF YOUR AUDIENCE

It's called "playing off your audience," and you must do it. You must not talk *at* them; you must talk *with* them. Too many people make a presentation as if they were in confrontation, nose to nose, one person yacking at the other. When you make a presentation, you should have the feeling that you have your arm around the other person's shoulder and you're talking buddy-to-buddy.

I've said that audiences are by nature courteous. But bear in mind that yours is probably not the only presentation the audience has listened to that day. Each presenter has no doubt promised miracles, perfection, unlimited service, and follow-up. Each one has cited success stories and incidentally (which the audience knows) omitted the failures. Haven't you found it disconcerting, after you've bought the best whatchamacallit on the market, to see listed in the instruction book all the places you can go to get it repaired?

Also, poor souls, they have been conditioned to hate meetings. Most of them have built up a defense mechanism, an invisible barrier against the excrutiating boredom they anticipate. They're sitting in a 75 percent fog. (Studies in the advertising business show that people who watch commercials on television recall only 25 percent of what's said to them.) How do you, the speaker, overcome this fog?

A story is told about the great comedian and actor Bill Cosby, who was hired to do a stint at a university. With him on the stage was a local dignitary, who got up to speak just prior to Cosby. The dignitary's speech went on and on and on. Everyone had come to be entertained by Cosby, and this selfserving pipsqueak kept talking and talking and talking until the audience started to get downright hostile. They shuffled their feet; they coughed; they shifted in their seats.

By the time Cosby finally came on, they were almost mutinous. But in just a few minutes, Cosby had restored their good humor, and he had their full attention. He had them in the palm of his hand. Years of experience dealing with people from stages of night clubs, where he was competing for attention with food, liquor, and conversation, taught him to develop techniques to cope with all kinds of audiences.

You've got to know your objective and be committed. You've also got to be personable. Talk to the audience naturally and warmly, and the barrier will come down. This is why performance skills are so important. In the theater we have developed techniques to cope with and to dissolve those barriers. I'll discuss those techniques in detail in the next chapter. Right now I want to discuss how you use yourself.

USE YOUR PERSONALITY POSITIVELY

Your style of communication, how you use your personality, is a strong factor in getting ahead. Numerous articles, interviews with CEOs, and management studies mince no words: your ability to communicate is one of the most important parts of the positive image of success. If you have reached management level, there must be something in your personality that makes you stand out from the crowd. Maybe it's your organizational ability, or your sense of humor, or your arbitration skills.

You've heard this before. Using your best skills naturally and unpretentiously is the best way to use your personality.

Before he became a movie star, the late John Garfield, who was then a member of the Group Theatre, was my first acting teacher. We called him Julie then. In exploring characterization, he drummed into us fledgling actors that we must avoid stereotypes. He and every other teacher and director I ever worked with reinforced the notion that there is no typical person. There is no typical soldier, husband, mother-in-law, farmer, or banker. Too many teachers of public speaking have the tendency to turn out cookie-cutter speakers. They stand the same way. They gesture the same way (if they gesture at all). And they phrase the same way.

The way to stand out is not to be a cookie-cutter presenter, salesperson, teacher, or preacher—dehumanized and formula-ridden. The way to stand out is to use your own unique, natural formula: yourself.

Incidentally, I presuppose that you're an expert. When you walk into a classroom, you have to have done your research. If you haven't done your homework, no one can help you. You must have worked out your rationale and your arguments; then you must say them in your own words.

One of my early clients was a top executive at an advertising agency. He told me of a situation in which his agency was competing for a prestigious automobile account. His team of top executives did everything according to accepted formula. They dressed resplendently and came loaded with success stories and an excellent marketing plan. They delivered

I have personally evolved—this is no discovery of mine, but I do talk a lot about it to my students—something that I refer to as the sense of self, the acceptance and use of your own individuality, no matter what part you may be playing. Now this sounds, perhaps, easier than it is. It's never easy to explain, by the way, because people insist on regarding it as some sort of a psychiatric formula—sense of self. I don't mean that at all. Really, it's a full use of your relaxed, easy state. It's the acceptance of yourself as an instrument.

—Morris Carnovsky, quoted in *Actors Talk about Acting*

their arguments with the utmost professional dignity. And they were commended by the potential client.

But, my client told me, the next man in was the president of a smaller agency. He was informally dressed, pulled up a chair, put his foot on it, and, after putting up a chart or two, said in a friendly, colloquial way, "When I got the ——— account two years ago, they had this share of the market. Here's where they are today."

My client didn't get the account; the second man did. The automobile account people liked him. He was the kind of guy you could fly cross-country with and not get bored. That and the obvious fact that he was one hell of a marketing man.

I have a horror of a performance becoming mechanical, automatic, and I watch like a hawk for signs of it. Then we try to find fresh lines, fresh ideas and emotions —new deliveries to make them spontaneous again. When you play your role just a little differently, it surprises your fellow actors and keeps them alive.
—Sir Laurence Olivier, quoted in *Famous Actors and Actresses on the American Stage*

BE ASSERTIVE

You've heard of assertiveness training. Theater people were the first to appreciate the value of being assertive. In a play each character is given a very definite objective.

Anna in *The King and I*: "I am going to get this barbarian king to respect me as a human being."

Iago in *Othello*: "I'm going to topple this foreigner off his high horse."

Hamlet: "Before I seek vengeance, I'm going to find out if my uncle really murdered my father."

How each character behaves and speaks is influenced and colored by each one's striving, despite obstructions, to achieve that objective.

To instill this assertiveness, we are going to do a series of exercises based on stalemate situations. The idea is for you to break the stalemate.

Unlike the real world, where you must communicate with honesty, courtesy and diplomacy, these exercises free you from these restraints so you can fully exercise your assertiveness muscle. I urge you to use your imagination, to be ruthless if necessary. The idea is to prevail, to checkmate your alter-character. In these scenes, go ahead and use any tactic to get your own way. You can threaten, lie, cajole, or pretend to be any kind of character (policeman, gangster, mayor, or doctor).

If you can get someone to work with you, that's good. However, these exercises were designed so one person can play both roles if necessary by physically moving back and forth (i.e., by changing positions as you change characters). This movement and interplay will render you much more flexible and will heighten the results. Try to meet each character's thrust and counter from the point of view of the opposition. Need I say you should find a nice private place for these exercises?

Sample Stalemate Situation

Two single men have been sharing a very desirable apartment for over five years. Just today both of them have gotten engaged to be married. One of the reasons their fiancées are willing to get married is the opportunity to leave a negative home life and move into this nice neighborhood.

Tom: Linda and I just got engaged, Harry.

Harry: What a coincidence, so did Rose and I.

Tom: We've been roommates for so long, I'm going to miss you. When can you move out?

Harry: What do mean, when can I move out? You're the one who's leaving. You know I've been paying the rent for the past two years that you've been unemployed.

Tom: That's my other news—I just got a new job today and I'll be able to pay you back all the money I owe you, with interest.

Harry: Great, you know this address. You can send the checks here.

Tom: My new job requires that I stay in this apartment. You see, I'm now with the FBI, and I have to keep surveillance on the Russian Embassy across the street. This is a matter of worldwide significance.

One of Edmund Kean's earliest acting teachers was Miss Tidswell, a Drury Lane actress. She used to place him before a portrait and tell him to talk to it, in saying his speeches. He was never to recite; he was to speak to someone.

—Helen Ormsbee, *Backstage with Actors*

Harry: Listen, I'm desperate. If I don't get this apartment, Rose will break off her engagement. If you don't move I'm going to shoot you with this gun.

Tom: Go ahead—then you'll never be able to collect the $50,000 I owe you. How will you be able to support Rose on the $5,000 you earn per year?

Harry: Okay, you're forcing my hand. I have here a picture of you making love to a blond. Linda, your fiancée, is a redhead. If you don't move out, I'll show it to her.

Tom: Let me see that picture. Now I remember that night. The girl I'm making love to is your fiancée, Rose. How can you marry a girl like that? If I were you, I'd join the French Foreign Legion.

You will notice the tactics used by both of the characters in this sketch. (It's written just as I improvised it; not a word has been rewritten.) Each man attempted to give the other a good reason for moving and didn't stand on his rights. The idea in these exercises is to be blatant, to go for the jugular vein. You really don't have time for the niceties. The idea is to out-think, out-maneuver, and top the other person. Don't worry about logic or believability. The idea is to make big waves.

Ellen Terry gave me the key, I think, to acting. She said, "Think of the purpose of the words and let the words pour out of your mouth.

—Lynn Fontanne, quoted in *Actors Talk about Acting*

Stalemate Situations

1. You are broke and are having lunch with a friend who's also broke. Each of you expect the other to pick up the check although you've both been bragging about your wealth. The waiter has just placed the check on the table. Without admitting poverty, get your friend to pick up the check.

2. You're one of two people on a street corner who spot a twenty dollar bill. You each step on part of it simultaneously. What do you say so you walk away with the money?

3. You are trying to talk your boss into giving you a raise at the same time he is urging you to take a cut.

4. You're one of two children of an impoverished king. For the good of the country, your father has requested that either you or your sibling volunteer to marry the rich but sixty-ish and dissolute ruler of a neighboring country. Get your sibling to volunteer.

5. You're one of two research scientists working on a cure for a dread disease. The cure has worked on animals, but now it needs testing on humans. The only people left for the test are you and the other scientist. Neither of you is too sure of the results of such a test and so wants the other to volunteer.

THINK POSITIVELY TO EDUCATE AND TO PERSUADE

At this point I want to remind you that I do *not* recommend confrontation or devious practices in real life. These exercises are purely for the purpose of developing the habit of thinking positively.

The best ways to motivate are to educate and persuade with honesty, courtesy, and diplomacy. Persuasion is probably better because people are highly motivated by self-interest. What would you think of an insurance salesperson who urged you to buy an expensive policy just to make a big commission? You'd throw that person out. But if he or she says, "This policy will protect you and make up for your losses if your house burns down," you're more apt to pay attention.

A good way to persuade is to use the word *you* a lot. In other words, you tell the person, "Here's what's in it for you." People are motivated by self-interest. Therefore "you" becomes a potent persuader.

Thinking positively about the other person and about yourself, defining your objective, and committing yourself to it will help you develop a natural platform style.

Indecision in acting Ellen Terry called a fatal quality. She had seen more than one good player ruin a role through not taking a firm grip on it—not deciding how to portray the character and sticking to this choice. To her, that was moral cowardice.
—Helen Ormsbee, *Backstage with Actors*

7

HOW TO USE PERFORMANCE SKILLS

You'll learn to use the uncomplicated Presentation/Performance Flow Chart for any kind of performance, whether you're selling Widget 36, working in a night club, preaching a sermon, or playing in Othello.

USE THE PRESENTATION/PERFORMANCE FLOW CHART

The flow chart shown here is what this chapter is all about. It's a flow chart of presentation and performance. There are five points. It's not complicated. And the flow chart applies to any kind of performance, whether you're selling Widget 36, working in a night club, preaching a sermon, or playing in *Othello*.

DEVELOP STAGE ENERGY

Please note this word *energy*! You've heard it referred to in different terms: stage presence, personality, charisma, pizzazz, electricity. The professional performer, just like the professional athlete, knows that this boils down to perspiration, to muscle.

We call it stage energy.

The first stage of any presentation starts even before you get up to perform. The first step is to psych yourself up to performance pitch.

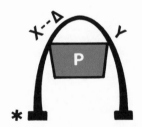

PERFORMANCE CURVE A

Look at the illustration of Performance Curve A. Sitting at the apex is the keystone: the presentation/performance. You say hello at point X. You say good-bye at point Y.

Most people start their presentation at point X. That's much, much too late. If you start your presentation when you get up to say hello, it's going to take you two to three minutes until the Δ to finally hit your pace.

I think energy, a good store of energy, is the real secret. Energy on stage is the real secret. Energy on stage is many things. In everyday life, energy makes us move with precision, whereas on stage, the more an actor uses excess energy and acts in a purely theatrical way, the more he blurs his objective and confuses his action. You create false notes when you overextend yourself.
—Constance Cummings, quoted in *Actress to Actress*

Presentation / Performance Flow Chart

1. Develop Stage Energy
   - Psych yourself up to performance pitch

2. Take Stage
   - Allow two seconds of silence to grab attention
   - Establish Rapport
   - Tell the audience the bottom line

3. Speak Eyeball to Eyeball
   - Create a one-on-one intimacy

4. Be Conversational
   - Keep it human
   - Tell 'em whatcha wanna tell 'em

5. Finish BIG !
   - Recap
   - Ask the audience to do something
   - Hold — one thousand... two thousand... three thousand... four thousand !

I've taught presentation skills a long time. In practically every class, I've heard, "Hal, improvisation isn't my bag." Or "I'm a systems engineer." Or "I'm an accountant." Or "Tell stories? I'm not an entertainer. Let me talk about what I know. I'm great at it. Oh, I may be a little off my feed, had a small fight with the spouse, but once I'm into it, I'm dy-na-mite!"

Then they invariably say, "It takes me two or three minutes to get there."

As a professional speaker, I know that you don't have two or three minutes. You have only thirty seconds. In two or three minutes, you have lost your audience. They have clanged shut their gates of privacy. You're talking about new software and they're thinking, "Why did Helen say that to me in the bathtub this morning?" All your words of wisdom are bouncing off an impenetrable wall.

When you greet your audience, you've got to hit your mark running full speed.

Now look at Performance Curve B. A presentation does not start at point X, when you say hello. A presentation starts at the foot of the curve, at the asterisk. That means a good half hour before you expect to be called.

Be prepared. Before I go on the stage, before I do an interview, before a Mike Douglas show, before I give a dinner, I'm prepared. To make it at the last minute is not how I do my best. Assemble myself, my dress, my jewelry or not-jewelry, my makeup, my hairdo, my thoughts, my anticipation, my dread, my inspiration, and when the cue comes, when the guest comes, when the director says, "Roll," I don't have to wait for inspiration, I'm ready. Go!

—Ruth Gordon, *An Open Book*

PERFORMANCE CURVE B

I'm going to draw the parallel of being a good speaker and being a good athlete over and over again. They have many skills in common. What pitcher would get on the mound without having been in the bull pen? What decent golfer would play in a match before hitting a bucket of balls on the driving range? When you see Larry Bird shooting baskets before the game, he is not there to enjoy himself; he is warming up.

You've got to warm up as a speaker.

What's the part of the curve past the keystone? It's follow-through. Same as golf: backswing—impact—follow-through. Same as tennis: preparation—impact—follow-through.

A presentation ends a half hour after you've gotten off the stage. Too many people end on the next-to-the-last transparency. They go into what I call the "thank God it's over" dive right there in front of the audience. Their whole effort can slide into the basement as illustrated in Performance Curve C.

PERFORMANCE CURVE C

You've got to give your audience the best that's in you: the filet mignon.

So the first stage is to psych yourself up, to learn what to do between the asterisk and point X, which I'll describe in detail in the next chapter. It's important now to talk about the skills you'll need when you're up there in front of the audience.

TAKE STAGE

You're introduced: "Hal Persons is going to talk about the new Widget 36."

You make your entrance, not in an invisible isolation

booth, talking to the carpet at breakneck speed, but as if you were in a spotlight. (By the way, you're going to feel like you *are* in the spotlight; I'll show you how in Chapter 8.) And as you go up front, you greet everyone in the room *silently* with your eyes. I repeat . . . *silently*. Greet the people on the right, those to the left, and especially those in the very back rows.

When an actor focuses on another person it helps him get out of himself.

—Eric Morris, quoted in
The New Generation of Acting Teachers

As you do that, say to yourself "What a good-looking group. Boy, am I glad to be here. This is going to be a terrific meeting."

You *must* say those words. Do you know why?

Look at yourself in the mirror. See how nice you look. I look nice when I do this, too. In fact, I look like a sweetheart of a guy.

Now people who've known me a long time know I'm mean. I kick little dogs. I race old women for the empty seat on the bus and win. But here I look nice. You know why? Because I'm smiling. And *you* look nice because *you're* smiling.

I don't care what course you've been to, your coach tells you "Why do you look so grim? Smile, baby." Right? So what do you see? You see people scared stiff out of their wits getting up before an audience looking peaked and hangdog but displaying all their teeth.

That's a cliche-smile. And, like most cliches, it's phoney. It's not a smile at all.

Now sometimes you don't feel like smiling. You've had this trouble at home, but you've got to smile. That's an acting problem. As actors, we learn that in order to project an emotion, like being happy, we've got to feel it. When you say these few magic words, "I'm glad to be here," they will make you feel good and you'll look good. Merely showing your pearlies isn't a smile. It's surface.

This gets right down to the quality of acting you take for granted in the movies and on television. When you see Dustin Hoffman or Sidney Poitier projecting anger, they're feeling anger. When Meryl Streep projects jealousy, she's feeling jealous. And when Sir Laurence Olivier looks happy and in love, he's feeling happy and in love.

In the old days, just before World War I, acting was

mechanical. That's what gave it a bad name. A book contained pictures of what an emotion was supposed to look like. When an actor needed to look frightened, he looked at the picture that showed what "frightened" looked like. Every actor did the same thing. That's why, when you see silent movies, you see all that phoney acting.

The modern realistic actor feels the emotion and therefore projects it believably. You want to smile? You've got to feel the smile. You've got to say the magic words, "I'm glad to be here. What a good-looking group. This is going to be a great meeting."

If you are really looking at them as you say this, you will actually feel a smile, because the real smile is an eye smile, not necessarily a tooth smile. The greatest smile in the world, the Mona Lisa, has lasted 450 or 500 years. You don't see her pearlies. Da Vinci just captured the smile in her eyes.

In verbal communication, your eyes are the most important organ. When you concentrate with your eyes, you'll hear. You sell, teach, and act with your eyes. You listen with your eyes.

Gesture and movement should come just normally right out of what you feel. You try to keep them as simple as possible. Sometimes when you see bad acting, you think, "If it's as hard as that to be good, I don't think I can be."

—Katharine Cornell, quoted in *Actors Talk about Acting*

Allow Two Seconds

I've been talking about this step for several pages, but do you know what I'm talking about in terms of actual presentation time? Two seconds! The first two seconds of your presentation is silent. We have a name for it: we say that you *take stage*.

The word *take* projects "I'm in command here. Pay attention. Achtung!" And your very bearing will project that.

In two seconds, you've succeeded in *grabbing the attention of your audience*. Until you see every eye on you, don't talk. Figure on about two seconds. It will seem like two hours until you get used to it.

Establish Rapport

While you have their attention, you want to establish a nice, friendly rapport with everybody there.

Don't charge in and say, "We have a very exciting announcement to make this morning." Don't plunge right in; make an informal remark. Maybe about the weather: "Gee, what a great day! Just like spring!" Or "How about that ball game last night?" Or, if you recognize a face, something like this: "Hey, Sherry, how are you? I haven't seen you since San Francisco."

What that says to an audience is "We have a human being here. Let's keep the gates of privacy open."

Tell the Audience the Bottom Line

Now, while you have them in a receptive mood, *hit them with your bottom line*.

The bottom line is important. It helps convince people in your audience they aren't wasting time by attending your meeting. You've got to tell people, up front, the purpose of your presentation. And the purpose is either to give information or to solve a problem. "What did we spend $2 million for last year?" "How will we market the new widget?" "Why haven't we made enough profit?" "There is a dearth of blood in the blood bank." "We need people to join the softball league."

Tell them what the need is. Then tell them what your recommendation is. Tell people what you expect them to do as a result of your presentation. Use the inverted pyramid construction of journalistic writing. Start with an attention-grabber, and then support your conclusions with ensuing information, as I will show you in Chapter 9.

Most of the time, the speaker says something like this: "My name is Hyacinth W. Blotte, director of mutual assistance for the Marshmallow Growers Mutual Protective Association. We concern ourselves with maintaining high mutual standards of production in the southeast agricultural area. I am here today to address the diminution of our membership's mutual aggrandizement in the last fiscal quarter."

By this time, everyone has clanged shut the gates of privacy and is settling down for a comfortable nap.

Here's the better way: "Welcome to Atlanta. You seem to have brought the sunshine with you to this meeting. We've had nothing but rain for the past two weeks. (Recognize some-one in the audience.) Harry Speer, how are you? Haven't seen you since the Cincinnati meeting. (Pause. Look around a bit.) Those stories on television and in the newspapers about the floods in North Carolina hit us where we live. Either they can result in great disaster or we can use them for the greatest advancement in the history of marshmallow farm-ing. Our research and development department has been developing an underwater marshmallow seed. With your help we can have a sufficient supply for sowing come April. (Then, introduce yourself if you were not introduced.) My name is Hyacinth W. Blotte.'' (Next, launch into your sup-port materials.)

Let me summarize the steps for taking stage:

> Look around (2 seconds).
> Establish rapport (4–5 seconds).
> State the problem (20 seconds).

So we're talking about thirty seconds up front to get the audience's attention and get people on your side so they will continue to pay attention.

Taking stage is an important part of performance skills. This is how a guy like Bob Hope can come up before a restless audience and get everyone's attention. Of course, he does it in his own style.

SPEAK EYEBALL TO EYEBALL

From the moment you say hello until the moment you in-troduce the next presenter, your eyes come into play. In verbal communication, your eyes are the most important organ.

Let me repeat. This is important. In verbal communica-tion, your eyes are the most important organ. Not your mouth. The tip-off is that you were given two eyes and only one mouth. What you've got to do is establish an *eyeball-to-eyeball* relationship with everybody sitting in that room.

I don't care if a person is twenty rows back or in the balcony. Each person in the audience must think you're look-ing at him or her from a distance of two feet.

The primary thing an actor learns to do is to connect with an object. The fact that I am looking at one of you, and connecting specifically with you at this point, delivers me from the interference of the other —of him who might be attempting to disturb my concentration. The more connected I am with you, the less I care about his interference.

—Morris Carnovsky, quoted in
Actors Talk about Acting

To accomplish this, you must eliminate from your very thinking that you ever talk to a *group* of people. Never talk to an audience. Never talk to a class. Never talk to a meeting. Never talk to a congregation. Never talk to the Kiwanis Club. Never talk to the PTA.

You talk to 1,000 people . . . one at a time.

Half a sentence to a person on the right. A sentence to a person on the left. A thought to a person in the middle. You visit a little bit to the right. You visit a little bit to the left. A half sentence. A full sentence. A thought. A visit. With practice, your instinct will give you your timing.

You must eliminate what you may have been taught elsewhere: scan the audience. Lord, Lord, don't scan. Don't scan because you can't kid people in an audience. They know you're not looking at them. You've got to go eyeball to eyeball. You must establish a one-on-one intimacy.

And you *criss-cross* the audience.

Some books say, "Talk to the clock in the back of the room." Forget it! You can't fool people in an audience. They know you're not talking to them.

Some books say, "Select one person in the room and keep talking to that person." It may help you, but that person wants to die of embarassment.

No. A little bit here. A little bit there. You see, it keeps people excited.

Some books say, "Look this way five seconds; look in the opposite direction five seconds." Audiences, if they're still awake, are a highly sensitized group of people, and they will notice things on the stage that they would never notice in any other situation. An actor, therefore, is essentially under a microscope. This could be intimidating, except that if the actor is himself or herself—if you are yourself—there's no threat.

But if you're regularly shifting your glances in a timed manner, the audience will catch that rhythm and shift with you.

When you criss-cross, you develop your own style. This does two very important things. First, it involves each person sitting out there. You see, a person hates being talked at. Each person, especially in corporations, hates the thought of being a corporate entity. He or she hates to be considered a number in a ledger. Remember, there's no typical manager. There's no typical vice-president. There's no typical wife. Each person has a life. Each person has a personality. Treat a person that way; then each person will stay with you.

And do you know who this mostly helps? It helps you, the speaker! That's the second important thing eyeballing does because you know moment by moment where you stand with the people in that audience.

There are two terrible things about speaking in front of a group: you're afraid of making a fool of yourself, and you feel isolated. It is not natural to be the only one talking. Except, of course, if you happen to be a politician. Communication is this: I say something, Joe says something, I say something. Right? Back and forth.

When you're up front, you may be the only one talking out loud, but people in the audience are going to react to you with their eyes. You'll create a dialogue. And they'll say things to you. They'll say, "I cannot follow these numbers as fast as you are dishing them out." They'll look confused. And nature will supply the answer: you'll slow down. They'll say, "Are you sure of that?" They'll look quizzical. And, if you have the proof, you'll trot it out right then and there. They'll say, "You turkey, you just insulted my entire ethnic group." If you didn't mean it, you'll immediately mend fences.

> *"Eyes, eyes! Your eyes are empty," Stanislavsky complained—for he knew that behind empty eyes is an empty mind.*
> —Helen Ormsbee, *Backstage with Actors*

This is why I strongly urge that you never memorize a presentation. Work from an outline so you have a lot of flexibility. For example, suppose that in order to make points with a group, you've selected a couple anecdotes about demon vice-presidents. But when you get up to talk, two vice-presidents are members of the group. So you change to anecdotes about presidents.

Once, when I was teaching at a major stockbrokerage firm, I noticed a young woman in the class turning green. I could see that nauseous look. And I said "What's wrong?" "I ate something that's not sitting right," she said. And I said, "Out." Now, she didn't want to leave, and if I hadn't noticed that, she would have disgraced everybody plus herself.

You've got to observe what's going on.

I tell you this because sometimes what you read in people's eyes is beyond your responsibility. People have private lives. The person out there listening to your report may have had a terrible fight with her spouse. Or he may have been up all night with a sick baby. Or maybe she has the flu. Or he may have flown in from Europe and has jet lag.

What do you do if the people who are important to you are distracted, chewing their fingernails, or looking at the ceiling?

First let me tell you what you don't do. You don't lean over close to them, snap your fingers, and say, "Hey, wake up!" Not only will you make an enemy of those people but you'll make an enemy of everyone in the room.

What you do is devote much more of your eye contact to those people. Five to one. Ten to one. But not all at once. Keep coming back. They will feel your gaze. And the chances are that these people will wake up and pay attention. And they will thank you, because you and I know how miserable it is to try to stay awake when your eyes turn leaden. That's the way to help such people. Another way is to ask them a question. Be sure you ask one that they can answer.

BE CONVERSATIONAL—KEEP IT HUMAN

If you eyeball your audience, the next step will follow: keep it human and keep it conversational.

Don't make speeches. Don't pontificate. Don't affect an orator's stance because you're up at the front of the room talking big bucks. The way you talk to your dearest friend in your living room is the way you talk to the president of the company, to the chairman of the board, even to the president of the United States.

Do not kowtow. When you are up in front, you outrank everybody in that room. Not only the chairman of the board but even your boss or your branch manager. And they want it that way. If you're great, they'll take full credit for your brilliance. You are the star. Or else they would be up here, or someone else would.

Do not gussie up your vocabulary. If you don't use polysyllabic words in your kitchen, don't use them anywhere. Five-cent words are so much more powerful. They give you an aura of authority. The words you use to talk with your dearest friend are the words you should use to talk about high technology or the theory of relativity. That should be your gauge. In some instances it will also help to see your friend's face—to imagine your friend's response.

Some people think, "Now listen, you're talking about technology that costs millions of dollars, so you've got to sound austere."

Baloney! Think of the great presenters you've sat in front of. Think of when you went to school. Which professors put you to sleep and which ones kept you awake? It had nothing to do with knowledge by itself. It had to do with knowledge plus performance.

Keep it conversational!

FINISH *BIG*!

Too many presentations just peter out . . .

They are ragged and insipid. A good ending can change a "No" to a "Maybe," a "Maybe" to an "I'll think about it," an "I'll think about it," to a "Yes." And a "Yes" to a "Let's go!"

To teach you how to finish successfully, I selected joke-telling as your practice presentation.

Remember, I told you earlier that the word is the actor's product. Do you know what an actor's income depends on? How much laughter, how much applause, he or she generates. The more laughter, the more applause, the bigger the income, the bigger the star. It stands to reason that performers have learned to milk a more positive response from an audience.

In show business, the axiom is Big Finish! Big Exit! *Big* is the key word.

Let me demonstrate how we create a big finish in the theater. It will work with "one-liners"; it will work with Lincoln's Gettysburg Address; it will work with Portia's appeal to Shylock; it will work with getting the powers that be to appropriate $7 million to build a new wing to the hospital.

For this demonstration I'll reach way back to the oldest routine I know: the "small room" routine. It's about the comic's complaints on the size room he was given at a hotel: "Small? (Pause.) That room was so small, I had to go into the hall to change my mind. (Pause.) It was so small, you couldn't laugh ha, ha, ha. You had to laugh ho, ho, ho. It was so small, I bent over to tie my shoelace, and I knocked down a wall. (Pause.) I called the room clerk and demanded a larger room, so he came up and scraped off the wallpaper. (Pause.)"

Where I've indicated a pause, the comic will not move a cell in his whole body. He will count four seconds, like this: one thousand . . . two thousand . . . three thousand . . . four thousand! Any kind of movement after a punch line will water down a positive response.

The presentation to the marshmallow farmers would go like this: ". . . So if we are to turn these floods into a bonanza for marshmallow farmers, we must get action immediately. We need your pledge for $4,000 each before this meeting ends! (Pause. Count four seconds: one thousand . . . two thousand . . . three thousand . . . four thousand!) Are there any questions?"

Until you get used to them, those four seconds can seem like an eternity. That four-second time period is called a dramatic pause. It ends your presentation with a great big exclamation point! Not with a question mark. Or worse, with a dot, dot, dot. A dramatic pause is natural and it works. It can double or triple your effectiveness.

If you watch television, you are subjected to this technique over and over. Stand-up comedians, singers, politicians, and dramatic actors apply the end pause consistently. In television situation comedies the pause is applied in two ways. After every funny line, there is about a two-second pause (usually covered by a laugh track). And instead of ending with "The End," as in motion pictures, the last thing you'll see before the credits is a frozen picture, called a freeze frame. The same freeze frame is used to end most television commercials because it adds clout to the message.

You learn the same technique in salesmanship courses. You are instructed to "Ask for the sale," which means "Ask them to do something." Then you're told, "Sit back and wait for your prospect to say something because the first person to speak, loses." Many a neophyte salesperson, anxious to close, will talk too soon and interrupt the person still considering the proposal.

You may not consider yourself to be a salesperson, but remember that a presentation is usually a sales pitch for something. Don't think you're not a salesperson. Each of you, from the receptionist to the chairman of the board, is a sales representative of your company.

To recap, look at the presentation/performance flow chart again.

8

HOW TO PSYCH YOURSELF UP
TO PERFORMANCE PITCH

You'll learn to project a positive, professional, glowing self-image by using exercise and imagery to develop stage presence.

Remember the performance curve? Now I'm going to tell you what to do between the asterisk and point X to get your energy flowing.

Why you do this is very important.

It evokes the word *professionalism*. A professional is someone who delivers beautifully come hell or high water. "Neither snow, nor rain, nor sleet . . .''

PERFORMANCE CURVE B

ACT LIKE A PROFESSIONAL

In the theater, we pride ourselves on our professionalism. We call it "being a trooper." You know the story: "I had appendicitis, but I sang the whole opera." The actor has got to be the ultimate professional. Why?

Because in the acting profession there are no such things as sick days, personal days, and until recently, paid holidays. In fact, we work on holidays. We don't play and they don't pay. You've heard the phrase "The show must go on." Now you know why. We need the rent money.

Actors have human problems. When traveling on one-nighters and when working in stock companies, the actor's normal state is exhaustion and the things that come with it, like upset stomach and colds. Yet that couple who hasn't been out in three months has hired a baby-sitter for the night and has bought two $30 tickets; they couldn't care less that the actor has a tummyache. Oh, they'll sympathize. They'll say, "Tsk, tsk." And they'll want their money back.

You can imagine how theater owners love to give money back.

Go back to Heifetz. His job is to play the Beethoven Violin Concerto as well as he possibly can for the audience that is in Carnegie Hall that night. Somebody else played it better; somebody else will play it better. But he's got to play it as well as he can, and above all he's got to love Beethoven and love the audience and love himself. If he loves those three people, he can't do wrong.

—Jose Ferrer, quoted in
Actors Talk about Acting

And another thing, working actors know that there are a thousand equally talented actors who would love to take their place in the show. At this printing, the actor's lot is not very secure. Actors' Equity Association, the actors' union, has a membership of over 30,000, 85 percent of whom are chronically unemployed . . . as actors. They may be waiters, taxi drivers, teachers, or word processors.

What do actors do if they would rather be back at the hotel with an ice bag and aspirin, yet they've got to show up at the theater and be funny, or dance, or sing?

ENERGIZE YOURSELF

The answer to that question is so simple you will not believe it until you've tried it. What I'm about to describe will sublimate your personal ills to the task at hand. The leaden heart will lighten. The racing mind will slow down. The nausea and fatigue will disappear. The aches in the joints will vanish.

Unfortunately, they will come back after the performance. However, because you energized yourself, the audience will be exposed to the best in you.

If you ever went backstage just before curtain time, you'd see the cast exercising: doing jumping jacks, push-ups, ballet turns, or pushing away from a wall. We call that "energizing."

Five or ten minutes of energizing will shape you up. You'll feel good. You'll feel bright.

How does this work?

We're dealing with two of nature's own chemicals. The first is oxygen. When you exercise you get more oxygen, which is an energizer and a tranquilizer. The second is endorphin, a chemical that exists in the brain and relieves pain.

I learned this from the head of psychiatry at a New York state hospital. She is a semiprofessional racquetball player. This woman told me that once during a match she broke her leg and didn't know it until about twenty minutes after the game was over. Endorphin!

Exercise will take care of you every time. You'll feel good. You'll feel sharp. You'll feel up. You can be great even when you don't feel like it.

Ideally, in the privacy of your office or the washroom, do about ten to fifteen jumping jacks or push-ups before a performance (before you take stage).

I can guess what's running through your mind right about now—you're calling me an ivory-tower birdbrain, right? You're thinking, "Sure, Hal. But suppose I've been at a meeting since 8:30 a.m., and two very boring presenters have talked the assemblage into a semistupor. Then when it's my turn, I stand up and say, 'Just a minute, folks, before I give my presentation I'm going to do ten push-ups here on the conference table.'"

No. Of course I'm not suggesting you do that. Everything in this book is geared to make you look natural. But with star quality. Star quality means being a trooper—ready to perform come hell or high water.

DO THE SECRET EXERCISE

Do my secret exercise and others won't know you're exercising. This is an isometric exercise, the same kind used by bombardiers and pilots on long bombing missions to keep themselves alert. By pressing one muscle against the other or against an inanimate object, you derive the same benefits as you do with more obvious exercise.

The secret exercise is this:

- Sit in a chair at the conference table or on the dais.
- Strike an informal stance. In other words, don't make it obvious that you're exercising.
- Press your feet firmly into the ground.
- Simultaneously, press your arms against your lap or against the arms of the chair.
- At the same time, press the small of your back against the back of the chair.

- Use this cadence:
  Press. One thousand. Two thousand. Three thousand.
  Hold it.
  Relax. One thousand. Two thousand. Three thousand.
  Hold it.
- Repeat.

Do not exercise your face. Others will give you a funny look. You've got to look comfortable. Otherwise it's a dead giveaway. What if your feet don't touch the ground? Cross your legs at the ankles and press them against each other.

Do this exercise a dozen times and you'll feel great. Do it two dozen times and you'll be flying. This exercise will cure whatever ails you. I've seen it happen time and time again.

RECOGNIZE WHEN YOU HAVE STAGE PRESENCE

I'm often asked, "How do I recognize that I'm at performance pitch? Is there a gauge?"

Someone wonders, "Suppose I start correctly, but after I've talked for twenty or thirty minutes, I feel my momentum slipping. How do I get back on track?"

Another person says, "What if someone suddenly asks me to speak. I go to the meeting for the free sandwiches, but then someone wants me to 'say a few words.' "

Use an Ancient Technique

You can use this technique when you find your energy ebbing during your presentation. You can also use it when you're called on unexpectedly.

Take an actor like the late Richard Burton playing Hamlet. It's a strenuous role because Hamlet is almost always on. Suppose in the last act Burton suddenly feels his energy ebbing? How does he get back on track? I can't answer that definitively because he had developed a technique of his own.

There is no performance that I do on this or any other stage which is not preceded by a moment, a curious moment, in which the door is unlocked, as it were. It's as if I say to myself, "Now, this is it. This is it." It's a kind of marshaling of all the resources.
—Morris Carnovsky, quoted in
Actors Talk about Acting

I know now how my work feels when it's right. I know physically how that feels. And I can recognize that feeling and get myself toward that nebulous state when I begin to work. It's a feeling like riding a wave. And sensing that rightness puts you, I think, in the right direction.

—Zeljko Ivanek, quoted in "The New American Actor," *New York Times Magazine*

. . . and I did begin to observe a curious trait shared to a degree by all [actresses], especially by those of a certain age. In fact, it seemed that the older that actresses get, the more they exhibit this mysterious phenomenon.

I am talking about the light.

I first really noticed it while talking with Dame Wendy Hiller when she described her meeting with George Bernard Shaw. I was particularly taken when she said he was surrounded by a blue light, and I remember doing a mental double take and thinking, but my dear, you are positively bursting with light!

—Rita Gam, *Actress to Actress*

But I'm sure it was a variation of an old, old theatrical technique we call "substitution," which is a physical analogy. You ask yourself, "What does stage presence feel like? What is similar?"

To me, stage energy feels like a glow. Like you're radiating. To me, a stage floodlight is the answer. Why a floodlight? Because a floodlight puts out 2,000 watts of illumination. It's bright. It's hot.

When you feel as though you're pumping out 2,000 watts, you'll feel on. You'll project stage presence! You'll have enthusiasm. You'll have authority. And you'll have star-like quality. You'll understand what it feels like to be a star. Like Frank Sinatra. Like the pope. Like the queen of England. Like Ronald Reagan.

You may be interested in how I came to relate enthusiasm to a glowing floodlight. I invoked one of the keystones of realistic acting technique. It involves using two helpers we get from nature—sense memory and emotion memory.

Consider this. When you project an emotion such as sorrow or anger, it's been stimulated by a current circumstance. You may not experience that emotion again for years. That's real life. But on the stage, which is only a reflection of real life, you must project that emotion on cue eight performances a week (including two matinees). If you're in a film and there are twenty-six takes, you've got to produce that emotion twenty-six times.

We know that our subconscious never forgets anything we've experienced. Here's an example of emotion memory. Have you ever recalled a really stupid thing you did? It may be ten years later, but you blush again. Or you remember how as a child your puppy got run over, and you cry real tears again. Actors use that kind of experience to condition themselves to really cry on cue eight times a week.

Want an example of sense memory? Picture an old-fashioned slate blackboard. Watch me scratch the slate with my fingernails. Did you feel a reaction? Yes, you did, yet there's no blackboard. But once you've experienced the reaction, your subconscious can call it up on cue.

There's another analogous technique called substitution.

This relates more directly to our friend, the floodlight. It's impossible to replay an experience like death. And it's nearly impossible to replay getting shot. Trying to experience those feelings can result in losing your job and in definite ill health. But actors play roles in which they die or are shot. So we try to find an analogous experience that might parallel the needed effect.

They say that in one play, Elia Kazan had to take poison. Of course, if he had taken actual poison, he would have been dead. So he tried to figure out what could possibly be a parallel. He took two uncoated aspirin and chewed on them. At the same time, he remembered once when he had a terrible bellyache, and he put the two of them together. It came out as "this is what it must feel like to take poison."

There was another famous actor, way back in the 1930s in Eva LeGalienne's repertory theater. His name was Jacob Ben Ami, a very fine actor. He was in a play in which he had to get shot. Now most people at that time said, "You get shot and you hold your hand over your heart and go 'uh!' He said, "It can't be that easy, it's got to have some kind of pain. I wonder what it feels like to get shot?"

He tried this and he tried that and he couldn't get it. One day, the hot water was turned off in his building, but he didn't know this. When he turned it on, he was splashed with a stream of ice cold water. He went "arghhhhh!" and he said, "That's it!" After that, every time he heard his cue—Bang! —he was in the shower. He so shocked the audience with his realistic reaction that there was five minutes of silence.

But it is easier for you, the speaker, because all you have to do is think about how it feels to be a floodlight and to glow.

Winston Churchill once said, "We are all worms, but I do believe that I am a glow worm."
—Rita Gam, *Actress to Actress*

Learn to Glow

So I'm going to ask you to act out the floodlight. It's a foot and a half high and ten inches wide. It's used to create sunlight on the stage. It emits 2,000 watts of illumination.

You're going to act out this floodlight. And in acting out this floodlight, you'll learn how to look in charge and how to actually be in charge any time you want.

Shelley Winters related how when once she did a television show with director Sidney Lumet, he asked her to "Come in the door, turn on the light, go over to the couch, and say your line."

"So I came in the door, I sat on the couch, and I said the line," said Shelley.

Sidney said, "No, Shelley. You come into the room, turn on the light, you sit down, and say the line."

"So I came in the door. I stood there. I sat down and said my line."

He said, "Turn on the light, dumbbell."

She screamed, "I did!"

Then she smiled at me and said, "I thought he meant my inner light, and I was turning it on."

—Rita Gam, *Actress to Actress*

It's an exercise in three phases:

Phase 1: Picture yourself as this floodlight.
Phase 2: Lights on! You are going to flare up to 2,000 watts.
Phase 3: Lights out.

Remember, this is internal. It's mental imagery. You cannot get up before the steering committee of the XYZ Ketchup Company, hold your hands over your head outlining a bulb, and tell them you have this new marketing strategy. They'll look at you funny. They'll call two people in white coats to come take you away.

This is an inner feeling. Don't do anything unnatural. Don't stiffen up. Don't pop your eyes. Be comfortable.

First, picture yourself as a floodlight bulb. Next, turn on the juice. Lights on!

Now, lights off!

Do it once more.

Lights on! This is what enthusiasm feels like. This is what charisma feels like. This is what it feels like to be a big star. This is what it feels like to be Sinatra. This is what it feels like to be the queen of England in her gold coach. This is what it feels like to be an Olympic winner receiving the gold medal. Lights out!

Learn to Relax

Acting like a professional and energizing yourself also involves relaxation. If you aren't relaxed, your energy remains

Reprinted with permission of Tribune Media Services

self-contained; it can't get past your stiff muscles. The brightest your floodlight can glow is 200 watts.

The kind of relaxation I'm talking about isn't the langorous kind you experience in the hot tub or after sex. It's exactly the opposite. This relaxation is the kind in which your muscles and your mind achieve super alertness through the absence of inhibiting tension, the kind of relaxation in which you know you can respond however you need to.

Telling yourself to relax won't work. Just like telling yourself not to be nervous doesn't work. Actors learn that it's difficult if not impossible to control (or wish) an emotion or psychological state. But they can learn to control the physical. They can control their hands, their eyes, and their muscles.

Saying to yourself "Pull yourself together" or "Shape up!" is useless. The harder you try, the tenser you become. The following physical exercises will help you every time.

USE FIRST AID FOR MUSCULAR TENSION

1. Tense all muscles, count to five, and release all at once. Repeat five times.
2. Breathe in—a long, leisurely breath through the nose —on a *slow* count of four. (1 . . . 2 . . . 3 . . . 4 . . .) Now hold the breath for a *slow* count of three. Make your jaw as slack as possible—lips relaxed, mouth open—and breathe out (almost a sigh) to a *leisurely* count of four. Then hold your breath for a *slow* count of three. Start again. This relaxing exercise should be done on a regular rhythm, as leisurely as possible. Repeat a minimum of five times. Ten times is better.
3. Sit in a chair or lie down on a hard surface (a bench or the floor). Begin by relaxing muscles easiest to control. Relax the muscles in your toes. Relax the muscles in your fingers. Relax your neck muscles. Check for tension in these areas constantly.
4. "Instant Relaxation": Use this technique if you're in a waiting room or other situation where you don't want to draw attention to yourself. Do the secret

Until you learn to completely concentrate through your whole role, you don't really play your best, or give the customers their money's worth . . . If there is any special secret to give as to concentration I would say that it lies in relaxation rather than pressure of intensity: the mind clearly divided between the imaginative impulse and the deliberate execution of the part, with nothing allowed to distract one from these two processes, which should be complementary—the one feeding and sustaining the other.
—Sir John Gielgud, quoted in
Actors Talk about Acting

This relaxation is the secret of good acting. Young actors when they are nervous tighten up as soon as they try to act. This tension sometimes is effective. But it is terribly exhausting and is only briefly effective.

—Sir John Gielgud, quoted in
Actors Talk about Acting

yawn: with slack jaw and relaxed lips, leisurely breathe in and then leisurely yawn through partially opened lips.

PROJECT A POSITIVE SELF-IMAGE

You project to others what you think of yourself.

My daddy told me, "Son, you don't have to brag. If you're good, people will discover it." For one of the few times in his life, Daddy was wrong!

In his book *Circling the Equator*, Mark Twain told a story about two men. One was the captain. He was brilliant, knowledgeable, and had the personality of a flounder. He projected such uncertainty, lack of knowledge, and diffidence that the passengers became concerned about whether he could bring them safely from Australia to New Zealand, even though they were in fact on the right course. The other man was a salesman. He was charming, dynamic, and ignorant. But when he pointed to a fork and said, "Use this to cut your hair with," the passengers believed him. That captain needed some of the salesman's brass. Everyone is born with the potential for star quality.

Now I'm not claiming that everyone has equal intelligence or equal talent. These are commodities that can't be taught. But just as all gold is not found on the surface, sometimes (too often) the gold—in the form of talent or intelligence—must be brought to the surface by removing a lot of crud.

To help you project the image that really represents you, you sometimes must use a lever to shoehorn yourself out of your shell. Nobody really benefits from having a shell except maybe a lobster.

You were born with the lever—the shoehorn—you need to extract yourself from that shell. It's called creative imagination. Please don't be frightened by that phrase. What I'm talking about is your ability to make-believe—to daydream, which, in turn, leads to the ability to cope with a problem, to troubleshoot, to invent, to innovate.

Thomas Edison was a creative genius; some say it took

him about five minutes to conceive of the motion-picture projector. He did all right in business despite being creative. I once read that Albert Einstein maintained that what evolved as his theory of relativity began years before as a hunch. Now a hunch is a creative impulse. This great scientist played a mean violin and loved gardening; neither interfered with his ability as a physicist. It's not sissy to be creative.

You have got to develop the courage to believe in your creative hunches (your instincts).

To stimulate your creative powers, you must begin by reactivating the capacity you had as a child to play cowboys and Indians, school, cops and robbers, and "I'll be the Mommie and you be the Daddy," and use it to your advantage in business.

We began this unleashing process way back in Chapter 3 when I talked about dissolving your cellophane wrapper and again in Chapter 6 when you worked with the stalemate situations. What you began to learn is that you don't have to walk on eggs when you speak. Venture! Tell other people what you think. You'll do fine if you keep in mind the three restraints: honesty, courtesy, and diplomacy. We assume you're going to do your homework. We assume you have the necessary expertise.

But bear in mind that being an expert is only the jumping-off place. Mark Twain's captain was an expert, but it wasn't enough to inspire the passengers to have confidence in him. Mark Twain's salesman had the flair but lacked the knowledge, so in the end he turned out to be an empty bag of wind.

What you must accomplish in business is to bond your expertise with the star quality you were born with. Unfortunately, society has beaten the star quality out of too many people. I'm talking about smart people. People with good incomes. And so when I counsel you to be yourself, I mean your optimum self. Your self the star.

When I get to this point in my workshops, there's bound to be someone who stands up and says, "Hal, I am myself. It's easy for you to be flamboyant because you're an actor. I'm a naturally shy and private person." I always wait for someone to say that. That sort of statement is what we in the theatre call a straight line—a cue for the point I want to

> *Julie Harris explained belief as being a 'sort of power of belief, a willingness to immerse oneself in the subject, whatever it is.'*
> —Rita Gam, *Actress to Actress*

> *Thus it is imagination directed by will that one is watching every time one sees a part superbly portrayed.*
> —Helen Hayes, quoted in *Backstage with Actors*

make to the person who said it and to you who are, at this very moment, thinking it.

Most actors didn't start out as the personable people you see on all those talk shows. In recent years, there's been an avalanche of autobiographies by stage and screen stars: Charlton Heston, Sophia Loren, Sir Laurence Olivier, Lauren Bacall. The thread that runs through all of them is how painfully shy they were as children. In the natural search for recognition, they found it expedient to perform not as themselves but to hide behind the masks of Cinderella, Romeo, Peter Pan, Falstaff, Othello, Scarlet O'Hara. Safely ensconced behind these masks, they thought, "Hey, it isn't me making a fool of myself, it's this other person."

The thing is, those characters didn't make fools of themselves. Quite the contrary: they were wonderful. The actors playing those characters got recognition and much more. They realized they could be wonderful without the mask. Voila! Celebrity! Talk show guest! For over twenty years I've seen this metamorphosis happen to inhibited business executives in two days.

Speaking of talk shows, I've been a Johnny Carson fan since he went on the air. Many's the time he's mentioned how shy he was as a child. His road to self-confidence was to perform as a magician, then on to stand-up comedy and stardom. Many, many comedians have taken the same route for the same reason. Incidentally, Carson maintains that he is still a shy and private person. You can believe it. But where it counts, he's a superstar.

In your private life you can be as shy and private as you want, but when you are being payed big bucks to move the world, you don't have that option. You've got to scintillate. Like any actor, you, too, can learn to scintillate. It all starts with upgrading your self-image.

You reveal your self-image by the way you stand, the way you walk, and the tone of your voice. Since visual impressions far outweigh any other, whether you like it or not, you are being judged, fairly or unfairly, by the way you carry yourself.

You can spend lots of time and money correcting your physical faults, but it usually isn't necessary to go to the expense. Since how you perceive yourself reflects in how you carry yourself, a change in attitude usually is enough to accomplish what's necessary.

If you are old enough to be attracted to the opposite sex, you have experienced what I'm referring to. I ask you, when are people their most magnificent? When they are courting, right?

Most people are at their zenith when they're on the make. If you're in love permanently or temporarily, you're warm, you're debonair, and you're witty. You even stand and sit differently. Put on a tux or an evening dress, and all of a sudden you've become somebody great.

You have got to stop thinking of yourself as Joe Nonentity or Joan Average. As I've already said, when you're making a presentation, you outrank everyone in the room, including the president of your company. And that's literally true.

One of the most valuable acting concepts we learned as student actors was this phrase: "The Magic *If*." It goes like this. If I were a baby, how would I eat this ice cream? If I were an old man . . .? If I were blind . . .? If I were drunk . . .? So with you, it's "If I were not a trainee but the president of this company, and all these people worked for me, how would I address them?"

Working with executives, I found an even more effective approach to improved self-image. It's the phrase "make-believe." It works wondrously well.

A slender, five-foot accountant attended one of my workshops. I told him to make-believe he was built like Mean Joe Green of football fame. Did he grow? Heck, no. But he came over as tall in the saddle. Napoleon was about five feet tall. I read somewhere that Judy Garland was less than five feet tall. I have always thought of her as being at least nine feet tall.

In one of the management consulting firms I've worked with, there was an ultra-reserved, very proper British woman. I couldn't get her to unbend. I asked her who she thought was the most gracious, most beautiful, most sexy actress she knew. She answered, "Katharine Hepburn." "Okay," I told her, "Make-believe you are Katharine Hepburn doing this

At Drury Lane, Edmund Kean made up, dressed, and avoided the greenroom where it was customary for the performers to assemble. He prowled about in dark corners of the stage, waiting for his scenes . . . In his isolation, Kean must have been drawing all his forces together, filling himself with that deeply-rooted concentration that can carry a trained, sure player over obstacles.

From his first entrance before the half-filled house, his triumph grew and grew through the play . . . When Kean realized that the audience "was going with him," as he later told his wife, he was filled with such immense excitement that he "could not feel the stage under him." It was a creative excitement, and it conveyed itself to the whole theatre. In the end there was shouting and cheering; his success was a sensation.

—Helen Ormsbee, *Backstage with Actors*

presentation.'' She didn't at all look or sound like the star, but wow! In one flight of the imagination, Lady Overly Careful became Ms. Glamorous Best-Self.

I could cite you hundreds of similar cases, but I won't. Make-believe you're the star, and you'll act like the star. Boris Karloff, in real life a gentle, intellectual man, made a fortune playing monstrous men in the movies.

I hope you've gotten the message. In business, in the professions, self-effacing stinks. In the armed services, we were cautioned never to volunteer because we usually got stuck with KP. In business I urge you to volunteer to make that presentation. The person who shoulders the responsibility gets the plum positions. If you want to rise in the business firmament, your supervisors must know you're there. And if you keep taking the back row, you're not going to get noticed. If you've been with the company a number of years, and they can't connect a face with your name or a name with your face, you'll probably get passed over when they come to hand someone the plum.

You can't get ahead on hot air. Braggarts and blowhards don't stay ahead for long. You must shine with your accomplishments, not by self-glorification.

My services are very often contracted by the human resources department of a company. I have many lunches with department heads. What I've heard from them over and over again is that one of the considerations for promotion is ''How recognizable is the person? How dependable is he (or she) in carrying out an important mission?''

When they think of you, do they say, ''Let's send Mary, she's great!'' Or do they say, ''Do you mean that of all the people we can send, the only one who's free is Mary?''

You can be the person they want to send. Be visible. Be yourself. Be your best self. Never settle for anyone less!

9

HOW TO ORGANIZE, WRITE, AND REHEARSE YOUR PRESENTATION

You're going to learn how a presentation will almost write itself with just a little shove and a minimum of anguish and wheel-spinning.

Let's return to square one. What happens between the time you're assigned to make a presentation and the time you get up and do it? You have to organize, write, and rehearse.

A presentation usually comes aborning on a Friday right after lunch. I don't know why this is. But it's usually a gorgeous day, and you've just come back from a nice lunch. You're looking out the window in your office and thinking "What dread disease can I contract in the next ten minutes so I can cut out and play some golf?"

Just at that sensitive moment, in comes Shirley, your manager, and says, "Lucille, you and I are going to Miami to do a presentation about the new XYZ system."

You say, "Shirley, I am delighted that I have been selected for this honor. All my life I have wanted to go to Miami to do this presentation. This is May 12 . . . let's see, with a little cramming and a little research, I should have something ready, oh, about December 29."

And Shirley says, "What do you mean, December 29? Lucille, I want you to meet me at the airport Monday morning."

You know what happens? Instant dysentery. There goes your weekend.

I have a name for your symptoms: "blank-page phobia" —the dread of putting words on paper. In this chapter, I'm going to show you that blank page phobia, like stage fright, is a needless state.

HOW TO AVOID BLANK-PAGE PHOBIA

I'm going to show you how a presentation will almost write itself with just a little shove and a minimum of anguish from you. A minimum of wheel-spinning. A minimum of sleepless nights.

To get this done, you need three basic tools. First, you need the original word processor—your basic pencil. Second, you need a data bank—such as a legal pad. Then, you need an ergonomically designed workspace—your kitchen table.

Ask Yourself Two Questions

Your first question isn't "Why me?" Your first question is "What is my objective in this presentation?" In other words, what does Shirley want you to accomplish? Write it down. "She wants me to suggest that we discard the Buttercup System and go to Tangerine 44." Write it down.

The second question is "Who am I going to be talking to —what kind of people?" In other words, who is your target audience? This is basic, necessary information. Are you going to be talking to data processing people? Are you going to be talking to top executives? Are you going to be talking to accountants? Management? Legislators? High school students?

Write it down. "I'm going to be talking to the City Council. My objective is to suggest that we discard the Buttercup System and go to Tangerine 44."

You must write it down.

Be aware of the objective as the target of your action. "I am going there. I know I am going there." Therefore, everything you do will relate to the final object."
—Morris Carnovsky, quoted in *Actors Talk about Acting*

Write It Down

You see, the anguish in writing comes from trying to keep everything in your head until you start writing. The anguish comes when you sit down at your desk and say, "What shall I say first?" That is a burden you don't need . . . yet! Deciding what you'll say first will come later. You've got to work from an outline. What I'm discussing now is how to get to the outline.

These two facts, *your objective* and *your target audience* become the bull's-eye on your target. That bull's-eye will keep you from going off in too many different directions. The way you talk to a person who just writes the checks is different from the way you talk to the person who created your acronyms. When you're talking to accountants, you'll speak one way if you're talking about changing bookkeeping systems and another if you're discussing how to detect theft. Knowing what your objective is and who your audience is will save you from a lot of wheel-spinning.

So now you must do a very simple physical maneuver. Sit in the chairs of your target audience and try to think about what questions they need answered in order to change from the Buttercup System to Tangerine 44. What objections will they raise? What graphics are you going to need for clarification? For support? And write the answers down.

"What's it going to cost?" Write down the answer.

"Why does it cost so much?" Write down the answer.

"What's wrong with the Buttercup System?" Write down the answer.

"I understand that Apple has a different . . . ." Write down the answer.

Whatever you think they're going to need to know, *write it down*.

There's something very important that you should know about this process—it isn't going to happen in logical sequence. So don't try to start from A and go to Z. You're going to think of things in the middle and at the end. You may think of twelve different ways to answer the same point. Write all twelve versions down. Do not edit. Do not throw anything away. Not yet.

Write it down.

While you're about it, write down what props you will need. Whatever you think of, write it down and get it out of the way. Now, you may think of something real dumb. Don't evaluate. Write it down anyway. "What I'll do is, I'll come in wearing my boxing shorts and I'll write "Surprise!" across my navel . . ." Now that's a dumb idea. But if you don't write it down it will keep coming back like a crack in a broken record and get in the way of better ideas. Write it down to get it out of the way. "I need airline tickets . . . chalk plus magic markers . . . flip charts."

You might, at this stage, get an idea for a graphic, so you make a little thumbnail sketch.

You may think of something which has absolutely nothing to do with the project, like, "Gee, did I defrost the turkey?" or "Did I leave my iron plugged in?" Write it down for the same reason: to get rid of it. The more you write down, the more selectivity you have. Get it down on paper.

Do not evaluate.

Even if it's a slight variation of something you've already said, write that version down too, because it could make a big difference. Right now, you're putting raw material into the hopper. Writing everything gives you more choices. Do not go half-cookie. Don't settle for the first idea just to speed up the process. It's more important that you gain your objective.

Write it down. Write it down. Write it down.

Use A Tri-fold

If you have time, take a piece of paper from a legal pad and fold it into thirds, as shown in the illustration.

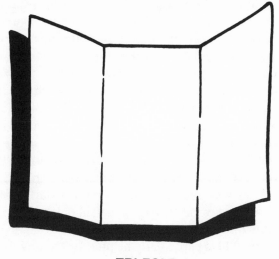

TRI-FOLD

Take this tri-fold and a pencil wherever you go until you're ready to sit down and put your presentation together. Take it to the party. Put it beside your bed. If you're going to mow the lawn, go shopping, or see a movie, take it along. Even if you're just taking out the garbage and that will take only fifteen seconds, take it along. Take it into the bathroom. But don't take it into the shower; it has a tendency to get wet.

Why carry this around?

Because you are dealing with your subconscious. And your subconscious has the greatest way of slipping you a flash

I also write out the lines in my own handwriting. Every night after we've staged a scene I come home and I write out— Stanislavsky recommended this . . . you know, the Russian actors didn't have copies of the plays . . . so they all had to write out their parts. And in a peculiar kind of way it becomes part of your guts when you write it out in your own handwriting.

—Shelley Winters, quoted in
Actors Talk about Acting

of inspiration when you're farthest from your desk. Very often, when I'm singing the second act from *The Pirates of Penzance* in the shower, which I do beautifully (no tickets available), I get this flash of inspiration, and I get out dripping wet and write it down.

Do you know why I do that?

Because if I don't, that idea will disappear into the void forever and never come back.

Many times, when I used to write television shows, I'd come back from a party and say, "Gee, I had the perfect one-liner, the perfect plot situation. But now it's gone." Write your idea down immediately.

So why this format?

This format gives you six great surfaces to write on vertically. You can write a short story, a lengthy short story, on one sheet of paper like this. Of course, this comes out of my experience as a New Yorker doing a lot of my creative work on the subway during rush hour. I don't like to waste time. So you see, you can hold it surrounded by garlic-breathing monsters, right?

It's useful, because you can't lose pages, and you can fold it and slip it into your shirt pocket, into your inside jacket pocket, into your purse, or into your jeans pocket. It's handy.

If you don't have anything as formal as this tri-fold, write your idea on whatever is available: a cocktail napkin, a Kleenex, a piece of paper bag, a matchbook cover. But *do* write it down because otherwise the idea is going to disappear. The tri-fold is particularly helpful, by the way, because it fits under your pillow. Don't you usually get a great idea just about the time you're falling asleep? If you don't write it down, you might forget it.

LEARN HOW TO OUTLINE

You sit down at your work station. You have several pads, pencils, and your tri-folds. When I sit down, I have a big pile of trash paper, predominantly cocktail napkins. There is something about the chemical composition of a cocktail napkin that inspires me. Very often, in my zeal I must dive into the nearest bar and order three or four martinis. I really don't like them, but I *do* need those cocktail napkins.

Now you are ready to begin the outline.

Get yourself some three-by-five cards. I like these because they're easy to handle. You can tear up a pad into small pieces of paper or cut up computer cards, just so the results are small. I like three-by-five cards best. They're easy.

Transfer one idea to one card. Write the whole idea out. If there are fourteen different ways of saying the same thing, write out fourteen cards. Don't be cheap with the cards. You'll see why in a minute. So you have everything: pads, pencils, trifolds, cocktail napkins, cards. The longer the project, the more cards of course. It stands to reason.

A word of warning here: don't throw the groundwork away until after the presentation. If you're like me, you might leave your final outline on the plane; if you've kept your cards, you won't have to go through the whole creative process again.

So transfer everything to cards. Sometimes I have a stack several inches high. I call this the "garbage-in" phase.

Now, you play solitaire. "This is what it's going to cost." "This is a market chart." "This is a psychographic table." Flow chart. Idea for transparency. Story from the *Wall Street Journal*. Alternate ad lib. History.

Lay your presentation out in categories, columns, or piles: Introduction, History of Product, Demographics, Cash Flow, Pertinent Legislation, Conclusion, Graphics. This is the first step in the editing process. Each category, column, or pile corresponds to the chapters in a book. Each card corresponds to the paragraphs.

When you have it all laid out on a flat surface, you can go into the second editing phase. I call it the "garbage-out" phase. Pick the best—the punchiest—and discard what isn't.

Ask Yourself: "How Shall I Start?"

Here we are in the middle of the chapter, and we're just now getting to "How shall I start?" "What shall I say first?"

> The finest hair line separates the good actor from the so-called "ham." The difference, nine times out of ten, lies in the power of selection, the ability to seize upon essentials and throw away the alluring temptations that clutter up a performance.
>
> —Katharine Cornell, quoted in *Famous Actors and Actresses on the American Stage*

Don't even think about how you're going to start until you reach this stage.

Now, you prioritize. (Even though most writing teachers will tell you there is no such word, that's what you do.) You ask yourself, "What shall I say first? Shall I start with this ad lib . . . no, I think I'll start with the *Wall Street Journal* quote . . . should I tell this joke? Yes, but later, after I talk about the graph."

Do you see?

Play solitaire. Prioritize. From card number one to the very last card, stack your argument for success step by step until you arrive at your call for action.

Put your beginning point on the left, and work from left to right. When you get through sorting and arranging, voila! There's your outline set out graphically. With a minimum of confusion. A minimum of wheel-spinning. A minimum of agony.

This is not a quick-and-easy method. It's not like instant mashed potatoes. You're still going to have to do research, requisition visual aids, and arrange props. The presentation won't automatically write itself. There is no *easy* way to do it. But this is the easiest. Some of you may have done term papers using this system. Incidentally, I didn't make any of this up. I learned this from the advertising business, where I worked hand in glove with the creative director, which is a fancy way of saying head writer.

Now, back to our data bank or, as it's sometimes commonly known, our pad. There are two ways of doing the next stage: the way I used to do it and the way I do it now.

What I do now is circle key phrases, numbers, and names on the cards, and then I make an outline. It's a little different from roughing it out.

I write:

1. Introduction (bullet, bullet, bullet)
2. History (A, B, C, D, E)
3. Cash Flow (etc.)

If you want, you can use Roman numerals for the major

headings. Or you can use Arabic numbers. Do this until you get it all down.

The way I used to do it in the beginning (and it's a perfectly legitimate way if this is the way you think) is that I used to write the whole thing out. Some people crystalize their thinking by writing the whole thing out. You don't have to, but if that's the way you organize yourself, great.

Organize for Success

I spent many years producing and directing television commercials. My clients were ad agencies. You always learn a lot from your clients.

Advertising is probably the epitome of communication media. On one page or in thirty seconds, advertisers must move mountains of product. And they do.

Count the number of print ads in a magazine. How do you get people to stop and read yours?

Now consider the plight of the television advertiser. Every station break there are six thirty-second commercials. Each commercial costs a huge amount of money to produce —between $50,000 and $1,000,000. The actors get residuals, and the air time is very expensive.

The advertiser competes with seven competitors. Five other ads all vie for your attention. The advertiser has learned to live with the five. The two the advertiser cannot tolerate are the refrigerator and the bathroom—two places most people go when there's a station break.

Advertisers have to figure out how to keep you in the room.

They've done so with a structure that's used both for television commercials and print ads.

ORGANIZE FOR SUCCESS
1. Use a grabber to get your audience's attention.
   - Actual
   - Hypothetical
   - Analogy
   - Media reference

2. Make your recommendation.
3. Support your recommendation with what the audience sees plus what it hears.
4. Recapitulate.
5. End with the clincher.

Use a Grabber

First, you need the "grabber" to get the audience's attention. It's also called a "hook" or a "headline."

■ *Actual.*   The best grabber is to talk about your audience's moment-by-moment concerns. Inform people they're not wasting their time listening to you. A presentation is usually given to address a problem: "We have not achieved our sales quota for this quarter." "We are not achieving our production quota because people are coming to work late." "We must cut down on travel expenses."

■ *Hypothetical.*   However, if you foresee a problem which you want to forestall, state the grabber as a hypothetical situation.

Imagine a fire-insurance salesman coming to Mr. and Mrs. Goldbucks' house. He looks around and then says, "Your house is beautiful. It must have cost you at least $150,000. And what lovely antique furniture you have. You must be very proud." He pauses: here it comes. "Mr. and Mrs. Goldbucks, if this house were to burn to the ground, would you have the wherewithall to replace it?"

More than likely this will never happen, but it could, and it stimulates the self-interest of the prospect.

Other hypothetical situations might be as follows: "Suppose there's a strike . . . ." "If your business keeps growing at its present rate, can you accommodate the customers?" "Suppose you have to appear before a stockholder's meeting?"

■ *Analogy.*   Here's the problem: the quality of your company's service isn't what it should be. You can introduce this problem with an analogy like the following one: "Suppose you were in a restaurant and the waiter was late taking your order. Then, when the food came, it was tepid and poorly cooked. That's poor quality. Would you go back? So, if our service is unsatisfactory, why should our customers come back?''

Abstract concepts are more easily understood when you explain them using common or universal experiences such as food, sports, and cars. For example, if you are talking about maintaining expensive computing equipment, you might say to a customer, ''If you paid $80,000 for a new Maserati and needed gas, would you take it to the generic gas pump? Or would you take it to that very special, super-duper, octane-rich pump?''

■ *Media reference.*   You can also use a news event as a grabber. This works because the event is already in the forefront of the news and audience interest is already piqued. For example, ''Did you see in this morning's paper that there was a power failure in New York City? It could happen in our town and cause a complete shutdown of our plant for days.''

Make Your Recommendation

Now that you have the audience's attention, make your recommendation. For example, ''I think it's imperative to purchase an electric generator as a backup system.'' State your recommendation in one or two sentences. Be brief. Be positive. Get to the point.

Support Your Recommendation

Now we get to the main thrust of your presentation, the various elements that led you to make your recommendation. Here's where you talk about cash flow, demographics, psychographics, case histories, project history, statistics, or whatever else it takes to convince. This is your area of expertise. Your information, based on experience, research, and judgment, is the strongest way to convince people that your recommendation is valid.

Be sure to back up what you say with graphs or other visual aids. What people see has ten times the impact of what people hear. In the next chapter, we will dwell on visual aids in great detail.

Recapitulate

Whether you've spoken ten minutes or an hour, recapitulate. It's another instance of the magic triad. The oldest formula known to motivators of all types is the old chestnut "Tell 'em what you're going to tell 'em. Tell 'em. Then tell 'em what you just told 'em." It works in teaching. It works in persuading. And it certainly works in selling.

Have you ever noticed that even if it's been a boring presentation, everyone snaps awake when the speaker says, "And now in conclusion . . ."? If people missed the message the first two times through, you're likely to score with your recap.

End with the Clincher

Finally, no matter how long you've spoken, if you do not ask people to support your recommendation with an action, you may have wasted a lot of time. No matter what you've been talking about, you have been trying to sell a concept or a product. Learn what is basic to people who sell—ask for the sale.

Ask people to volunteer. Ask them to appropriate. Ask them to join. Ask them to approve. Ask them to set the next meeting. Ask them to buy. Ask them to do something!

If you're playing Hamlet and your fly comes open, that doesn't help your concentration on "To be or not to be." See that that zipper works before you start, see that the codpiece snapper stays snapped. Acting is inspiration and preparation. . . Get inspired and learn where the chair and door are.

—Ruth Gordon, *An Open Book*

REHEARSE OUT LOUD

Now we come to rehearsal. And what I'm about to describe is the equivalent of the first time you told your funny story. Did your story hang together? Does your presentation hang together?

Think it through and mumble it through.

The mistake most people make is that this thinking it through silently or mumbling it through is the closest they ever get to a rehearsal. No matter how many times you do either, it's not a rehearsal.

You've got to hear yourself say it out loud. All great presenters rehearse: Winston Churchill, Ronald Reagan,

Johnny Carson. Why does your ear have to hear what your eye reads so well?

Because we have been taught to write for the eye, for reading.

But when you do a presentation, you are writing for the ear. It's completely different. What reads well may sound archaic, stilted, or downright awkward. You've got to be conversational, right? You've got to hear yourself speaking your presentation out loud.

There are two ways of doing that. You go into a colleague's office and say, "Norman, I have this three-hour presentation on the psychological implications of sleeping at your desk. I have fifty slides, and I have transparencies plus a few cassettes. Would you listen to me rehearse my presentation?"

You already know what he's going to say. "Hal, I'm delighted. All my life I've been waiting for the opportunity to hear your three hours of presentation. But in about five minutes I plan to have malaria." And he heads for the coffee shop.

You're not going to get anybody to listen to you. (Let me warn you: do not rehearse in front of your spouse or sweetheart. It's instant divorce. You'll break your heart with the effort you're putting out, and he or she will come up with something pertinent like, "Don't wear that color shirt with that jacket. It makes your face look pasty.")

Be practical. You've got to be your own director.

What you do is beg, borrow, or steal a cassette recorder. Then, working from the outline (if you've written the presentation out, reduce it to an outline), speak your talk out loud into the cassette recorder.

Listen to yourself.

But listen to yourself from the point of view of your target audience. If your presentation needs a little punching up, it won't take much time to polish. You've done the lion's share of the work already. Polishing is going to take a relatively short time.

If you think your target audience is really going to be motivated by what you've said, go! But be sure to time the

Stanislavsky said that the actor rehearses to make habits. First he decides what habits he wants to have, then he rehearses to acquire them, which means conditioning himself by doing it repeatedly until it's a habit. Then the whole performance becomes a habit. In the last phase of rehearsal you make all the habits beautiful. Ultimately, acting is also an aesthetic consideration. It has to look aesthetically pleasing.
—William Esper, quoted in *The New Generation of Acting Teachers*

tape. If you were told to talk for twenty minutes and your presentation lasts an hour, you've got to cut it down.

By the way, the shorter a presentation, the better. I don't think a presentation of any kind should be more than ten minutes, but I'm a voice crying in the wilderness.

FOIL MR. MURPHY'S LAW: BE YOUR OWN DIRECTOR AND PRODUCER

Put together your graphics and all the props and work with them so they work easily, so you won't fall into any of Mr. Murphy's traps.

In a presentation, you've got to be not only your own director but your own producer. The buck has to stop with you. If you depend on anyone else, it's going to be you up in front of the group with egg on your face.

You're a professional, and if you're sincere and unassuming, an audience will give you every break. But if you look like you haven't done your homework, they'll put you down. An audience will not tolerate amateurism. So check everything out.

As your own producer, beware of two phrases.

The first phrase is "Of course." "Of course Zebra Widgets has a working overhead projector." Not necessarily. "Of course there's a functioning lamp in the overhead projector." Forget it. "Of course they have an outlet on the same side of the room that I want to be on. And if they don't, of course they have an electrical extension." No way.

Check it out. Check it out. Check it out.

Use a pre-presentation checklist. The more you do the same presentation, the more you've got to use the checklist. I'll tell you why.

Two years ago, I showed up in Detroit with everything except shoes. I was dressed in a suit, shirt, and tie, and had to use my desert boots. They're pretty but they just don't fit. Before I leave now, I ask myself, "Do you have your shoes? Do you have your ties?" I go over my checklist.

Always go over your checklist. The more you teach, the more you present, the more you need a checklist.

PRE-PRESENTATION CHECKLIST

Rehearse
A. Speak out loud
B. Use graphics and props

Stage-Manage
A. Reconnoiter the room
    1. Seating arrangement
    2. Light switch
    3. Electrical outlets

B. Check equipment and props
    1. Graphics
    2. Clean film/slides
    3. Projector (extra bulb? gate clean?)
    4. Tape recorder
    5. Easels
    6. Electrical extensions
    7. Mike on?
    8. Screen ready?
    9. Props
    10. Pointer
    11. Push pins
    12. Masking tape
    13. Index cards
    14. _____
    15. _____

Anticipate
A. Set up graphics for easy handling
B. Use tabs
C. Color code where appropriate
D. Number everything
E. Have correct film reels, recording tapes, slides, etc.
F. Have film splicing cement, patches, splicer, and tape

The other phrase to beware of is this: "Don't worry."

If someone tells you "Don't worry," worry a lot. Other versions of "Don't worry" are "It's a piece of cake" or "No problem." "No problem" may equal "Big problem."

Check it out yourself. Be very careful. Ask yourself, "Did my secretary pack the carousel? Is it the right carousel? Are all the slides right side up?"

YOUR MEMORY IS IN YOUR HAND

One more thing—notes. A lot of people feel far more comfortable if they have what we call in television "idiot cards."

I strongly recommend that you don't put your notes on a big pad or a big piece of paper because people's eyes will be glued to the pad and not on your face. It's a natural habit of the animal kingdom, and humans are animals, to look at the bright, shiny object that is moving in front of them. They can't help themselves; it's involuntary.

For instance, when I teach people to appear on television I say "Don't wear a diamond stickpin or diamond necklace, or even diamond earrings. Don't wear shiny objects. Keep accessories muted so that the audience will look at your face and not at the shiny object."

For notes I recommend three-by-five cards or something similar. They are handy. They can be held in the palm of your hand, stuck in your shirt pocket, or placed on the table or podium. Hold the cards in one hand so you'll be free to gesture with the other.

Do not write sentences or use script. Print a word, a name, a number. Print block letters a half-inch high so you won't have to squint to read. This will act as a flow chart through your presentation. Print with a heavy marker so that the words are easy to see. An acronym, a name, a number is all you need to remind yourself of what you want to talk about for the next five minutes. Don't forget, all the stuff you have on the flip chart and on the overhead projector also acts as a flow chart.

Whatever you do, if you love yourself, do not write flor-rid prose in longhand across a card. Because you have seen it happen and I have seen it happen. "Members of the City Council, the most important thing that you must consider in this new technology is . . ." The presenter glances at his card, can't read it, and buries his face in it in order to get the information that will make his most important point.

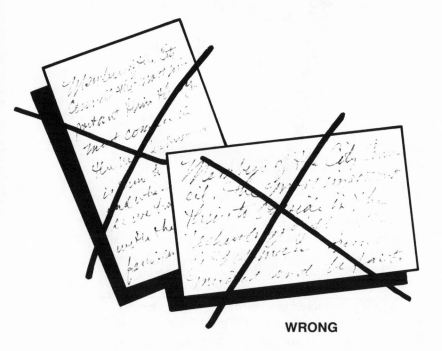

WRONG

You wrote it, it's your handwriting, and you can't decipher it. Do you know why? Adrenalin is flowing, and when adrenalin is flowing, there's a different kind of eye focus. Something that makes perfect sense in your living room or on the plane becomes garbage when you're up in front of a group.

A name, a word, a number on the three-by-five card: that's all you need as a reminder to see you through your presentation. No more than four items per card. Number each card.

More than likely, you'll never need the cards. They are

RIGHT

like the parachute on an airplane—there if you need them. Be careful. Don't let them become a crutch. However, they can be reassuring just before the meeting when you think you've forgotten everything you're going to say. (They're handy to rehearse with on the plane, too.)

One last suggestion. There is a time to write things out completely. If you have a lengthy quote, don't try to memorize it. It's perfectly legitimate to whip it out at the right time and say, "Now in 1939, Tom Watson said at the meeting in St. Louis . . ." You just pick it up and read it. That's perfectly all right.

10

GRAPHICS: VISUAL AID OR VISUAL CONFUSION?

No matter how professional, how exciting, how charming your delivery, a well-done visual image will help you waste not a thousand words and will help your audience better understand and remember your message.

Why do advertisers use illustrations? Why don't they just buy space and say "Our brand of aspirin is better for curing headaches"? Why do they go to the expense of showing a photograph of a man or woman, usually very handsome, first suffering and then smiling with relief?

THE EYE REMEMBERS LONGER AND DEEPER THAN THE EAR

Long ago, the Chinese were the first to say that one picture is worth a thousand words, that the eye remembers longer and deeper than does the ear.

No matter how professional, how exciting, how charming your delivery, a visual aid will help your audience retain your message and understand it better.

In Chapter 5 I told you that research has helped confirm that what people see has eight times the impact of what they hear. It breaks down like this. What they hear is 7 percent of the impact whereas 38 percent of the impact is voice quality, and the rest, 55 percent, is the visual impression.

That's pretty interesting stuff, isn't it?

Again, as I did in Chapter 5, let me give you the same information in graphic form.

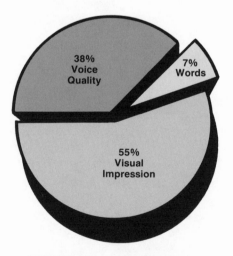

PRESENTATION IMPACT

Doesn't this graph make the proportions stand out?

To illustrate the importance of the audible part of your presentation (7 percent), I used the graphic analogy of the automobile engine.

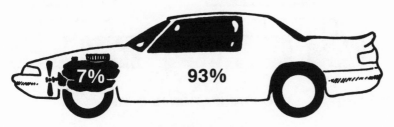

**KNOWLEDGE MAKES YOUR
PRESENTATION GO;
PACKAGING SELLS IT!**

The automobile graphic is a way of engraving on your mind that, although the nonverbal portion of your presentation outweighs the impact of the verbal portion, without your knowledge and logic, your presentation won't go. But most people still buy the car for its looks rather than for the motor.

The looks of the automobile can be compared to your appearance—how animated you are, how much enthusiasm and warmth you project, and how you're dressed. *You* are the most important graphic up there. Visual aids are to help you emphasize and clarify what you are saying.

For example, if you're talking about the organization of a company, you can say, "The president is Jack Jones. Reporting to him are Sam Snell and Nancy Black. Reporting to Sam are Mary, Harry, and Lois. Jim and Ruth report to Nancy."

Of course, this information is somewhat understandable because you are reading it. Imagine if you were hearing this material; wouldn't you be thoroughly confused?

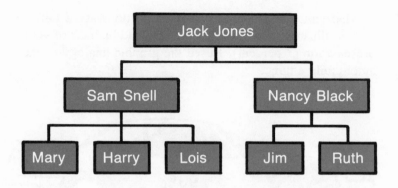

ORGANIZATIONAL CHART

But when you show your audience this information using an organizational chart, it's more clear. Visual images help people understand and remember. A picture helps you not to waste a thousand words.

Suppose you want to tell people at a meeting about your survey. You can say, "Our survey shows that 15 percent of people prefer bubblegum-flavored ice cream, 20 percent prefer wild blackberry, 60 percent prefer chocolate cookie ice cream, and 5 percent are undecided."

In choosing a visual aid, you can use a printed chart like the one shown. This is an improvement over just saying the figures. It underlines the statistics and makes them clearer and more memorable. But it doesn't really dramatize the true significance of the various percentages.

PEOPLE'S ICE CREAM PREFERENCES

- **15% Bubblegum**
- **20% Wild Blackberry**
- **60% Chocolate Cookie**
- **5% Undecided**

Now look at the same information in graphic form.

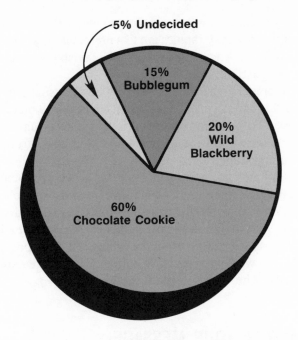

PEOPLE'S ICE CREAM PREFERENCES

Visual aids are most effective when they are used to enhance the spoken word. They must emphasize, illustrate, and clarify. Visuals add dramatic interest. Colored visuals are even nicer.

ALL GRAPHICS ARE NOT EQUAL

DON'T LET VISUALS TAKE OVER

Visuals give added impact and clout to what otherwise might be boring statistics. Graphics are to a presentation what spices are to cooking. And as in cooking, too lavish use can really prove indigestible.

Remember, when we are talking about visual aids, the key word is *aid*. You're using visuals to help you meet your objective. To let them dominate is to create visual confusion and distract your audience's attention away from you and your message.

Visual aids are not a substitute for a live presentation. Too many presenters get carried away and use visuals as a substitute for their performance. Some actually read slides or charts with their back to the audience. That's just a half-step better than sending around a memo. And the presenter wouldn't be wasting everybody's time. The picture explains the words. The words explain the picture.

DRAMATIZE YOUR MESSAGE

Just because you're right and just because you've said it doesn't necessarily mean that the audience has heard and re-tained your message.

Take a leaf from the books of advertisers. They engage in advertising *campaigns*. They repeat their message over and over again. They broadcast their commercials frequent-ly on many stations. In the average thirty-second commer-cial, they repeat the name of the product at least three times. I call this the Magic Triad. The Reverend Jesse Jackson's speeches are a good example of how effective the Magic Triad can be in oratory.

You must repeat your message often. Teaching requires repetition. Effective advertising requires repetition and so does motivational speaking. A presentation is used primari-ly to motivate.

The television commercial you see on the air has cost

the advertiser an enormous amount of money—usually in the millions. Both the advertiser and the agency want to know if they are getting enough bang for their bucks. By the time sales figures come in, they may have spent a fortune on a bummer. So they conduct surveys.

One system is to send a team to a shopping mall. You may have seen them. They are usually very handsome young people clasping a clipboard, hovering near a large trailer. They invite you into the trailer, give you a free sample of the product, show you a commercial, and then ask you questions about the commercial.

One conclusion resulting from these surveys is that people remember only 25 percent of what they hear. People's attention spans are short. They have personal concerns. They may have colds. They may have had an argument at home. A spouse may have had a headache. And, all too often, the presentation is boring. That's why, to overcome this tendency of the mind to wander, you must build lots of excitement into your presentation. Professionals don't call a presentation a "dog and pony show" for nothing. Be witty. Be animated. Use graphics!

Dramatize! Dramatize! Dramatize!

NET OUT YOUR GRAPHICS

In my long association with IBM, I learned a very valuable phrase: net it out. This means to rid your message of unnecessary fat. This sage advice applies in particular to graphic support material.

When people read and listen simultaneously, their concentration is diffused. In addition, they can't read as fast as you talk. Since the powers of concentration are mostly in the eyes, what you have to say will suffer. So to make a stronger visual impression, use only key phrases and words.

If possible, use simple pictures, drawings, maps, and graphs. Avoid using full sentences. And even in using phrases, cut out the fat. Take out *the, this,* and *but.* The ampersand (&) is usually a great substitute for *and*. Don't say "In order to meet our goal." Say "To meet our goal."

Sometimes you are stuck with a pre-packaged slide. Help people focus on what you want them to see by underlining key phrases with colored ink.

People have a tendency to read ahead of what you're saying. To keep their eyes focused where you want them when you're using an overhead projector, obscure the material that's to come by placing a sheet of paper over the transparency and sliding it down as needed.

If you're using a busy slide or flip chart, help people focus by pointing with a pointer to the phrase you want them to read.

LEARN TO USE SOME POPULAR VISUAL AIDS

There are a number of visual aids on the market. My preferences are these:

1. Flip chart—up to 25 people
2. Overhead projector—one person or more, depending on screen size
3. Slides—one person or more, depending on screen size
4. Chalkboard—up to 40 people

Films or videos are super for demonstrating a product, a procedure, or "before and after" examples.

Flip Charts

Until the advent of the viewgraph, flip charts were the most popular medium for inexpensive and flexible graphics, small or informal meetings, and writing while you talk. Flip charts are still a very good tool in small, informal meetings—particularly if you must create your graphic as you talk.

(These presentations are referred to as "speak and squeak" presentations.) If you must travel with flip charts, however, keep in mind that they are cumbersome and bulky.

When you write on a flip chart, use block letters one and one-half to two inches high. If your writing isn't legible, or if the audience in the back of the room can't read your chart, you might as well have no chart at all. Dark and heavy (bold) is easier to read than thin and light. Always use a thick marker. Favor dark colors—black, blue, dark purple, red, or green. Stay away from yellow, orange, violet, or pastel colors.

Even when you write as you speak, really lean into your marker and exert a lot of pressure on each letter. Take the fraction-of-a-second longer to *print* each letter. That slight retard will result in a bolder, neater letter. Although it will seem like it's taking forever, there will be scarcely any difference in the time. Writing with pressure works even if you use script, which I still don't recommend.

They are called flip charts because you flip pages as you go from chart to chart. To avoid fumbling as you flip pages, make tabs from masking tape and stagger them as shown in the illustration. Of course, if you are really rich, you can purchase packages of tabs from commercial stationery stores.

MASKING TAPE TABS

Put these tabs on either the left or right side of the flip chart, depending on where you plan to stand. Since English is written and read from left to right, I personally prefer to stand on the right and put the tabs on the right. People who write Hebrew or other languages that are written from right to left usually stand to the left.

Another method of tabbing is to fold the corner of each page, staggering the folds by making the longest fold on the bottom page. You can keep your tab folded flat with a staple or by tearing and folding as illustrated.

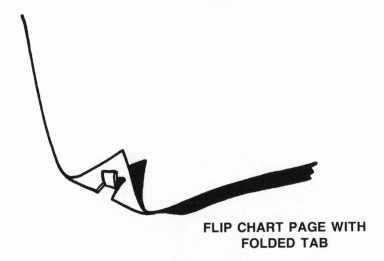

**FLIP CHART PAGE WITH
FOLDED TAB**

To prevent your next graphic from showing through, allow a blank page between charts. On all graphics, don't crowd too much material on the surface. Leave lots of white space. On flip charts and transparencies, there should be a minimum of three inches of margin all around.

The Overhead Projector

The overhead projector is a very flexible, convenient, quick, and inexpensive way to create graphics.

The housing (A) contains a light source. When you place your transparency on the glass platform (B), the graphic drawn there is projected onto a periscope (C), which reflects the graphic onto the screen or the wall.

The graphics are duplicated on an 8½-by-11½-inch sheet of acetate film. These films are called acetate slides, acetates, viewgraph slides, transparencies, or foils. I will refer to them as foils. The beauty of the foil is that it can be as simple or as lavish as you want. A machine called a transparency-maker will transfer practically any artwork from the original to the foil.

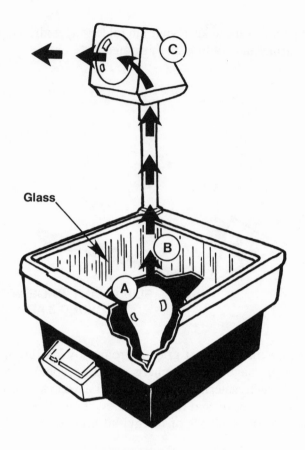

Glass

OVERHEAD PROJECTOR

What I said about graphics in general is also true of this potentially helpful piece of hardware. Overhead projectors can be important visual aids when used well, but they can be a bane if used incorrectly. I see things done by prestigious presenters that make me want to cry. I cry a lot.

Staging Your Overhead Presentation

When you're positioning the overhead projector, consider both your audience's needs and your own. Set the projector cater-corner so that everyone in the room can see without someone's head obscuring the screen.

If you have a fixed screen, try to tilt the beam so the

image is above everyone's head and as near the top of the screen as you can get. If your screen is a blank wall, shine the image as close as possible to the ceiling. Sometimes this results in some distortion of the image (i.e., keystoning, which means the image area won't be a perfect rectangle), but this distortion is preferable to obscuring your graphic from the people in the back.

POSITIONING THE OVERHEAD PROJECTOR

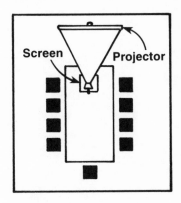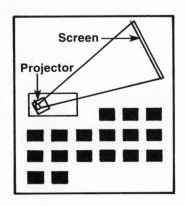

OKAY   BETTER

When setting up your projector, allow space for two stacks of foils. Decide on a pickup place and a discard place. And if you're going to use a foil again, allow for a repeat stack. If there's not enough room on the table, use a chair, bench, or typewriter table.

Before the meeting, provide your overhead with a Dallas Shutter.

"What the heck," you ask, "is a Dallas Shutter?"

First I'll tell you *why* you should have a Dallas Shutter. The image on the screen is designed to help you, so when it has nothing to do with what you're talking about, the image is distracting. You should turn off your projector. Because the switch is usually located toward the bottom of the housing, the audience sees you constantly diving for the switch.

Some projectors have a tiny, old-fasioned toggle switch that makes turning off the bulb even more complicated. Furthermore, turning the bulb on and off frequently decreases its life, and the bulb is likely to blow in the middle of your presentation. (Use your pre-presentation checklist; make sure you have a spare bulb.)

The Dallas Shutter, invented by a genius somewhere, is simplicity itself. It's a piece of cardboard cut to fit the front of the periscope and taped to the periscope with masking tape. When you want to obscure the image, you flip the cardboard over the lens. When you're ready for the next foil, flip the shutter back with your forefinger. It's fast. It's convenient. It prolongs the life of the bulb.

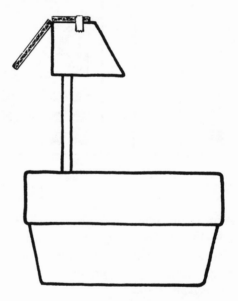

DALLAS SHUTTER

Why do I call it the Dallas Shutter? I first saw it used at a workshop I was conducting in Dallas. I was going to call it the Instantaneous Digital Image Obscurer Thing, but I didn't like the acronym IDIOT.

Oh, one additional thing! If you have one of the Neanderthal-era projectors (and some are still around), the strong lenses with which they're equipped may cause the cardboard to burn. Simply wrap your cardboard with aluminum foil to eliminate that danger.

You've set up your meeting room, positioned the projector, and affixed your Dallas Shutter. Now you're ready to begin.

It's Show Time!

The opening procedure of your overhead presentation is as follows:

1. Floodlight on!
2. Holding your foils in a very business like way, stack them on the pickup spot.
3. Check to see that the Dallas Shutter is in place.
4. Turn on the projector.
5. Place your first foil on the projector platform. (You haven't said a word yet.)
6. Step away from the projector and "take stage." Now you can begin to talk. If at all possible, never take stage from behind anything—a desk, a podium, or the projector.
7. Do the "reveal!" As you are about to show your first foil, step back to the projector, flip up the Dallas Shutter—*voila!*—and proceed!

Changing Foils

When changing foils, too many people do it very awkwardly. They remove one foil, causing a blast of light from the screen, before putting the next foil in place. This flash is not a sin; at most it's discomforting. However, there's a better, smoother, more professional way. We borrow a technique from motion pictures. Instead of jumping from scene to scene abruptly, motion pictures dissolve from scene to scene for a nice, smooth transition.

With an overhead, effecting a dissolve is a simple procedure. Here's the way to do it:

1. Anticipate that you need to change foils.
2. As you continue to talk (no meaningless pauses), with one hand grasp the foil to be removed.
3. With the other hand pick up the next foil.
4. Place the new foil directly over the first foil.
5. Slide out the first foil and place it on the discard pile. *Voila*! Dissolve!

Remember, you continue to talk all through this maneuver, unless, of course, there is a justifiable need to pause. This technique is not difficult. With just a few minutes of practice you'll be able to change from one foil to another with style and grace.

Additional Things To Remember

Because of static electricity, the acetate sheets tend to adhere to one another. Some people recommend a sheet of paper between each foil. That works, especially if you've creased the paper to lessen the vacuum. However, using paper gives you something more to handle between changes—remove paper, place on discard pile, pick up foil, put on overhead platform, etc. It's an extra maneuver you really don't need.

I suggest you use the cardboard frames available in any stationery store. They preserve the life of your acetates, and they render the use of an extra piece of paper unnecessary. If they are not available, I've found it effective to firmly press your four fingers toward the bottom of the foil and slowly slide the acetate toward you until it's free enough to lift and place on the overhead.

To help align your foils when placing them on the overhead, affix a pencil or ruler at the top of the glass platform with masking tape. This is a simple and effective jig and will cut down on fumbling and fussing.

Point to words or pictures on the screen, not on the foil itself. The manufacturers of overhead projectors give as one of their selling points that you can point to whatever you're talking about on the foil. Yes, you can, but *don't*! Pointing on the foil can obscure the screen from a number of viewers because you're in the way. Pointing on the foil also ties you down to the machine. It inhibits the free use of your body language. You can't look your best when you're hunched over the foil pointing. You lose eye contact. Don't do it.

Always bear in mind that you are the most important ingredient in your presentation. Anything that will render you less animated is counterproductive. If you must point, point on the screen.

The best pointer is your finger. If you can't reach what you want to point to, use a pointer. When you're not actively pointing, put the pointer down.

When you need to point, stand to the right of the screen, face your audience, and point sideways with your left hand. Sometimes it is necessary to stand to the left of the screen. That's okay, but point with your right hand—the hand nearest the screen. If you use the other hand, you'll have to point across your body; you'll be looking at the screen and you'll lose eye contact.

Glance at your screen just long enough to know where to place the pointer; then turn to face your audience and continue talking.

Sometimes, to dramatize a point, you may choose to write on your foil in front of the audience. (Using the overlay technique described later in this chapter is preferable.) But let's say for one reason or another you decide to write on the foil. If you're going to use that foil again, place a blank foil over it before the meeting and write on that. You'll be able to discard the write-on afterward.

What to Put on the Foil

What I'm about to tell you applies to any kind of slide or foil. Since the graphic is meant to emphasize or clarify the main points, it is counterproductive to put your spadework on the slide. You don't have to show the sales figures for as far back as 1893 when only this year's figures are relevant. That will result in an overly crowded slide and just confuse your audience.

Remember, in graphics, less is more effective.

If only four items out of forty are relevant to your objective, make a slide showing only the four pertinent items.

However, if you believe that the spadework figures would be helpful in getting a positive decision from your audience, put that material in a printed handout to distribute as the audience leaves. Never, *never* give people anything to read while you are talking. They will inevitably be reading page 10 while you're talking about page 3.

Don't Mix Apples and Oranges

Coordinate what you are showing on the screen with what you are saying.

If you're talking about apples, show apples. If you are talking about oranges, show oranges. If you're talking about oranges and are showing an apple on the screen, that could be confusing.

Limit the number of words on a foil to as many as you can say in one breath. Even then, stay away from using sentences at all. Use just the pertinent phrases in that sentence. Eliminate connective words wherever possible, as shown in the illustration.

— 57 percent of the patients using our program live to 92.

— 57 percent of the patients using our program live to 92.

57 %
live to 92.

LIMIT THE NUMBER OF WORDS

Computer Graphics

Thanks to the blessings of modern technology, producing colorful professional-quality graphics has become readily available to all. Most computer companies have developed the capacity on some of their machines to turn out highly interesting color foils. If, for one reason or another, you don't have that kind of technology available to you, I want to tell you how to make a pretty effective and professional-looking foil without having gone to art school.

Do-It-Yourself Graphics

First, let me tell you what not to do. Because of the ease of duplicating, too many people have a tendency to take a memo or letter, rip a page out of a catalog or proposal, and slap it on the transparency machine.

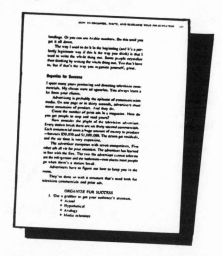

BOOK PAGE AS TRANSPARENCY

For example, the transparency shown in the illustration was taken directly from a book. Now if that isn't the epitome of visual confusion, what is? Pages from books and typed documents have print letters and illustrations that are too small, too complicated, and too crowded. Therefore, they are impossible for the audience to read. You'd be better off without that foil or slide; it's counterproductive.

However, if you must indeed use typewritten material, use a typeface specifically designed for typing speeches. To me, typewritten graphics are the choice of last resort. They are too cold and lack pizzazz.

DISPLAY WRITER

GIVES YOU

THE MOST FUNCTION

FOR YOUR DOLLAR

GOOD

Compare the typed words with hand-lettered words. Handlettering is more dynamic. You can experiment with colors and various letter styles. You'll also be able to space the words more advantageously.

DISPLAYWRITER:
Gives you
the MOST FUNCTION
for your dollar.

BETTER

As good as hand-lettering is, compare it with the next version.

This one is more interesting, of course, but, equally important, the illustration will engrave itself more indelibly on your audience's memory. That's why a soap advertiser not only prints the name of the product but spends a fortune to supply a picture, so you'll recognize and be sure to buy that brand and not another.

BEST

Even though I'm not sitting there with you, I can read your mind. You're thinking, "I thought you said I could do this without being an artist."

Well, the young woman who designed the foil with the drawing wasn't an artist, either. She went to her magazine rack, found an appropriate illustration, laid a foil on it, and traced. I've done this kind of thing over and over. Not only am I not an artist, I have two left hands, and they're all thumbs.

All over the world, commercial artists are turning out artwork for you to borrow once or twice—material in magazines, comic books, children's coloring books, and catalogs. But be careful. For more than casual use, whether you choose famous comic characters like Mickey Mouse and Garfield or drawings drawn by your neighbor and the president of your company, you must get permission for their use from the copyright owner.

What do you do if you don't have a magazine handy? One person used a styrofoam coffee cup to create some eye-catching abstract design like that in the illustration. Even an abstract design heightens interest by adding style and sophistication.

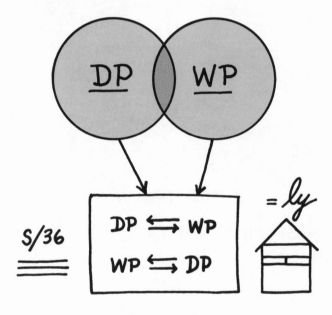

INTEGRATION

Do give your graphics production value. Don't be afraid. You don't have to be dull and boring. Even if no one at your company has ever done it that way before, people will welcome the excitement of well-planned and visually interesting visual aids.

Do you remember the graphic I used in Chapter 7 to illustrate the flow chart of performance skills? Look at the illustration here to refresh your memory.

Presentation / Performance Flow Chart

1. Develop Stage Energy
- Psych yourself up to performance pitch

2. Take Stage
- Allow two seconds of silence to grab attention
- Establish Rapport
- Tell the audience the bottom line

3. Speak Eyeball to Eyeball
- Create a one-on-one intimacy

4. Be Conversational
- Keep it human
- Tell 'em whatcha wanna tell 'em

5. Finish BIG !
- Recap
- Ask the audience to do something
- Hold — one thousand... two thousand... three thousand... four thousand !

Having read what I've just written, you'll be justified in thinking, "Hey! That's too busy. Too much information on that foil. It goes against everything he's suggested."

You're right. But there's more to that graphic than meets the eye. I thought it necessary to use a flow chart format to explain performance skills, but the class didn't see the whole of this visual aid all at once. The material is not on one foil. What you see is actually five foils. I used a series of overlays to build up the graphic to dramatize my story.

I took five blank foils, some masking tape, and a cardboard foil frame. (If you can't get the frame, this will still work.) The idea is to put only a small section of the flow chart on one foil. When the foils are placed one over another, information is presented bit by bit until the entire flow chart is complete.

I'll show you Foil 1 first.

*Hide not your talents.
They for use were
made.
What's a sundial in
the shade?*
—Benjamin Franklin

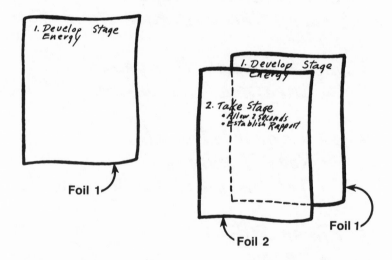

Foil 1

Foil 1

Foil 2

Foil 2 contains all the information under the heading "Take Stage." When Foil 2 is placed over Foil 1, the "Take Stage" information appears beneath the words "Develop stage energy."

Foil 3 contains the "Eyeball to Eyeball" material, and so on. Stack all the foils together and check them to make sure the lettering doesn't overlap.

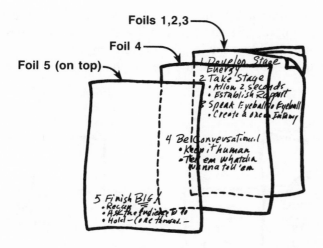

STACKED FOILS

The next step is to make a "booklet" out of the stack of foils. Center Foil 1 on the cardboard frame. Tape it to the frame with clear plastic tape. With additional tape, make a hinge on the left side of the frame and attach Foil 2. Hinge each additional foil the same way until you have finished the booklet.

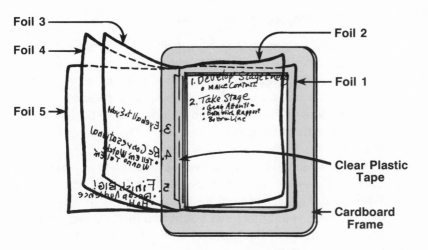

FOILS IN BOOKLET FORM

Overlays are particularly effective when using graphs. For example, instead of presenting an entire pie graph on one foil, build up the graph gradually by using a separate foil for each section of the pie graph.

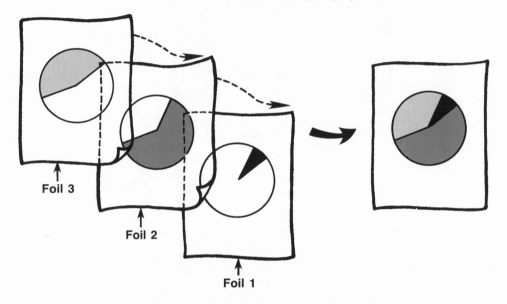

STACKING PIE GRAPH SECTIONS

Off-the-Shelf Prepackaged Visual Aids

More and more corporations have their own departments that turn out computer graphics. A whole industry has sprung up which prepackages audiovisual presentations. Several of my students have complained of having a package of a hundred slides or foils dumped on their desks with the instructions to use them in their presentations. The students complain that there are too many slides or foils.

If someone gives you a kit with a hundred tools, do you have to use every tool on every occasion? Of course not. When you're given a prepackaged deal, take only those slides that will help you. Sometimes you'll find that you need only about 25 percent of the package. If the slide doesn't clarify or underline your message, don't use it.

Slides

Slide presentations are increasingly popular—for teaching, for community relations, and for product sales promotions.

What I advised about overhead foils applies as well to 35mm slides. Because these slides are so convenient and portable, there's a potential overkill problem. Carousels have a capacity for 100 slides, so you are furnished with 100 slides when 12 might do a much more effective job.

The slides themselves are often overcrowded with words and images (much too much for a person to read in a reasonable time) and therefore lead not to clarification but to confusion.

The ingredients of a good slide are as follows:

1. One idea per slide.
2. No more than three lines per slide.
3. No more than five or six words per line.
4. Images that are easily understood.
5. Simple, bold type.
6. Color.

If the objective of your slide presentation is to motivate, educate, or clarify, don't ever use a multislide presentation. Multislide presentations dazzle. They entertain. They impress. But they also confuse. One slide at a time provides a minimum of distraction.

Eliminate the bad habit of allowing a slide to stay on even though it's irrelevant to what's being said. Black slides are available to insert in the carousel at the appropriate places to eliminate this distraction.

Where are you when the lights go out?

This is a trick question. During a slide presentation, there is a tendency to turn out the lights. Unless you shine in the dark, don't do that!

Never turn out the lights. The audience will not be able to see you. And remember, you are the most important element in your presentation. Also, with the lights out, too many people could seize the opportunity to catch forty winks.

If the lights are so bright that it's difficult to see the image or the color values, dim the lights. If there's no dimmer, turn out the lights, but hunt up a couple of desk lamps and train them on yourself like a spotlight. Take a hint from movie theaters. They always have some light.

Chalkboards

My least favorite graphic medium is the chalkboard or dry marker board. Of the two, I lean toward the dry marker. You can write more legibly, use color, and erase less messily.

My objection to both is that you usually have to put all your material up ahead of time. Also, it's difficult to dispose of material you no longer need. You can, of course, erase as you go, but that interferes with the continuity of what you're saying.

If this is the only medium available to you, here are some helpful hints. Picture different sections of the board as different slides, and allot different sections on the board to different graphics. Draw lines between the different sections.

Always print large and bold. Here's the way to get thicker letters from a piece of chalk. Hold the chalk at a forty-five degree angle from the chalk board. Grind it at that angle until you've achieved a very broad point.

CHALK WITH BROAD POINT

To prevent the chalk from snapping, hold it as close to the writing end as possible and write using firm pressure. You can color-code different areas of the board by using different-colored chalks. Color also helps clarify graphs.

If you are going to use complicated diagrams, it's best to do them before the meeting. Cover them with paper until they become relevant.

If you have to talk and write at the same time, raise your voice as you face the board. If you're writing quite a bit, glance over your shoulder at your audience frequently. If you do find it necessary to erase, keep talking as you do so. It will help maintain continuity.

If you drop a piece of chalk, pick it up because people are expecting the crunch.

USE SOME DRAMATIC GRAPHICS

Sometimes you don't need graphics to make a point. For instance, if you're talking about the amount of information that can be stored on a floppy disk, you can compare the actual disk to a two-foot high pile of paper.

If you're explaining why your company is grossing billions but has only a small profit, you might pull an apple from your pocket, take a bite and say, "This is labor costs," and take another bite and say, "This much is for taxes." Or you might slice a pizza to show labor costs, taxes, shipping, and materials, leaving those slices in the box. You might hold up the final slice, say, "Here's what's left for us," and cut it into small pieces for your audience.

A POSTSCRIPT ABOUT PODIUMS

Too many people consider the podium the most important element in a presentation. That attitude can be compared to a person who thinks the life preserver is the most important thing on an ocean cruise. Such a person uses the podium, not as a visual aid, but as a crutch—something to cling to for support in moments of agony.

I would like to start a great big bonfire fueled solely with podiums. That one piece of furniture has done more to emasculate and depersonalize multitudes of speakers than any other thing.

The podium was invented to meet a very real need. A place was needed to hold the Bible. The Bible is a very heavy book and taxed the strength of the poor clergyman who had to hold it throughout an hour-long church service.

To be realistic, I can't burn all the podiums. And if I could, I would earn the hostility of the podium industry and they wouldn't buy this book. Besides, that's where the microphone usually is.

If there's a podium on the scene (and there usually is), let me tell you how to prevent it from depersonalizing you.

First, *ignore it*! Stand to the right of it. Stand to the left of it. Stand in front of it.

A young woman who had taken my course was a junior executive at a very prestigious public relations firm. She was invited to address the graduating class of the high school from which she had graduated. Sure enough, there was the podium center stage. The principal, the mayor, the congressman, and the clergyman all spoke from behind it. Shortly, there was a lot of coughing and foot-shuffling in the audience—a sure symptom of boredom. My student, as she was taught, ignored the podium and, notes in hand, walked in front of it. She spoke for only ten minutes. She moved to the right and she moved to the left. The audience gave her an ovation!

Buck Rogers, formerly corporate vice-president for marketing at IBM, ignored the podium. He was and still is considered one of the world's great presenters.

Second, *distance yourself from the podium*. If, as is often the case, the podium is sandwiched between two banquet tables, here's what you do.

Stand at least a foot away from it.

Don't center yourself behind it. Stand near the right or left corner, allowing at least half your body to be visible to the audience. This positioning results in more dramatic staging. What's involved here is a basic principle of design. An asymmetrical composition is much more dynamic than a symmetrical one. Symmetrical is tame, placid, and has a tendency to be boring. Asymmetrical composition has a good deal more punch, as you can see in the illustration.

There's another advantage to this kind of staging. It gives you the opportunity to casually cross from one edge of the

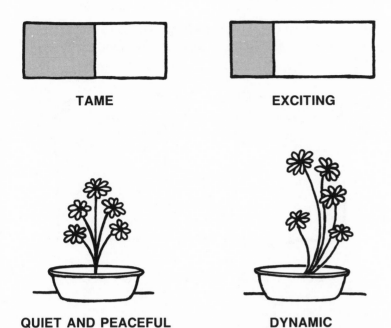

TAME **EXCITING**

QUIET AND PEACEFUL **DYNAMIC**

podium to the other during your presentation to effect a stage cross. In this case, the cross is only two or three steps, but, as on the stage, it gives people in the audience a booster shot of interest because they view you from a new perspective.

Third, *don't grasp the podium*! Don't lean on it. Don't even touch it. You want to be free to talk with your hands. Tying them up with the podium prevents that. You don't need to be propped up. You don't need a life preserver. Far from helping, the podium (if touched) acts more like an anchor.

Finally, if you read, *use the podium positively*. As you'll learn in the next chapter, you'll read when you have a press release or when you think you might be misquoted. You'll also read legal documents or financial reports. The podium is a handy place to put your script.

Incidentally, if you need glasses to read, put them on before you begin.

To go from one page to the next, use this broadcasting method. Broadcasters want to avoid the rustle of the paper as they change pages. So instead of turning pages over, as with a book, they place their scripts on the left side of the podium and simply slide the pages to the right when it's time to go to the next page. It's a good idea to fold the upper right-hand corner of each page to facilitate grasping the finished page.

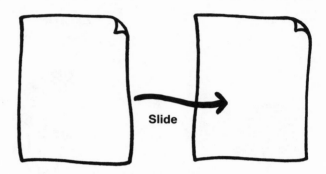

**SCRIPT POSITION: WHERE TO FOLD
AND HOW TO SLIDE**

I have seen Queen Elizabeth II of England without a podium hold her speech in her hand to read. As she finished one page, she slid it underneath.

11

TO READ OR NOT TO READ, THAT IS THE QUESTION

When reading is necessary, we in show business have developed a system that helps you mark your script for smooth delivery so it doesn't seem as though you're reading at all.

As I've stated previously, the best way to keep a presentation natural and dynamic is to work from an outline. However, there are occasions when reading your presentation is necessary.

These occasions include any situation where you're reading for the record and do not want to be misquoted, misunderstood, or misinterpreted:

1. Press releases
2. Position papers
3. Complex financial reports
4. Complex stockholder reports
5. Synchronized slide presentations
6. Voice-over film commentary
7. Someone else's report

In all the above instances, it's still a good idea to start with some informal remarks to establish rapport. It is ridiculous to see a speaker read, "Thank you, Mayor Smith. Good morning, ladies and gentlemen. Welcome to Chicago."

The problem with reading is that too many people read their presentations in a mechanical, monotonous, wooden way. They sometimes put emphasis on the wrong word. They phrase awkwardly.

There is a method that can help even the most inexperienced person to read a presentation as if he or she isn't reading at all. All it takes is a little practice.

REMEMBER RADIO DRAMAS?

The system was developed—where else but?—in show biz. In the days before television, there were some wonderful dramas, sitcoms, and soap operas, such as Lux Radio Theatre, Amos 'n Andy, Archie's Tavern, and Our Gal Sunday. Actors stood around the microphone and read their lines from the script. Rehearsal time, especially for daily soap operas and commercials, was limited—sometimes to as little as half an hour. To ensure that their performances would coincide with the director's instructions, many actors developed a system of marking their scripts.

With the advent of television and popularization of the documentary film, the cost of production shot into the stratosphere. Again, the less time taken in rehearsal the better, so "voice-over" announcers use this same system to mark their scripts. ("Voice-over" refers to *seeing* a picture while *hearing* only the announcer.)

In recent years, many people have employed the teleprompter to help them read naturally. However, the equipment is expensive and therefore not too practical for an ordinary meeting. But teleprompter scripting is very useful and can be exceedingly helpful.

I'm going to show you how to mark (or "score," as in music) your script using both methods.

LAY OUT A SCRIPT FOR SMOOTH DELIVERY

In marking or scoring your script, use a soft pencil, the kind used for drawing (HB #3) so you'll get a nice, heavy, bold line. This pencil is better than a pen because if you want to make a change, it'll be easy. And, because you'll probably be making lots of changes as you practice reading, it's advisable to have a large eraser handy. To begin with, mark your script lightly. When it's more or less set, make your marks heavy.

Score Your Script for Naturalness

The chart shows examples of symbols that you can use to score your script for a natural delivery.

The markings for breathing are self-explanatory. It is important to always have enough breath support to ensure that your voice doesn't peter out at the end of each sentence, making it impossible for your audience to hear those last few words.

Winston Churchill used to say, "Never stand if you can sit. Never sit if you can lie down. And never miss the opportunity to go to the bathroom.'' When you are speaking, never, never, never miss the opportunity to replenish your air supply with a catch breath or a full breath. Always speak with your lungs full of air. Your voice will remain positive and pleasant.

The musical bridge indicated in the phrasing section of the chart serves the same purpose as in music. Certain phrases must be delivered as if they were hyphenated. To ensure that they are delivered that way every time, use a bridge. A bridge is also useful to indicate other kinds of word groupings based on meaning.

Through the years I've run into typists (that's what word processors used to be called) who, no matter how many times you tell them neat margins do not matter, must produce neat margins. So they break up a phrase by shifting a word to the next line or, worse still, break up a word by hyphenating it. Of course, sometimes your lines on a typewriter or computer aren't long enough to hold all the words of a phrase or a sentence. To remember that the thought is continued on the next line, extend your bridge well into the right-hand margin, as shown in the sample passages on the chart.

Underlining is another useful device. Underline the words you want to emphasize.

To cue yourself for a slide or flipchart change, use the symbols shown on the chart or make up your own. If you really want to get fancy, use the musical symbols for louder and softer.

Don't, if you love yourself, gook up your script with instructions in the form of words such as "loud," "soft," "point," "change slide." Such instructions could interfere with the continuity of your delivery. In extreme situations, you could even mistakenly read them into your speech.

For best results, read your script out loud while marking.

Type the Script for Easy Reading

Following are several differently marked versions of Lincoln's Gettysburg Address. The only difference between the first two is the spacing; one is double-spaced and one is triple-spaced. Notice how much easier it is to read the triple-

SCORING CHART

Breathing

/   short pause   catch breath

//   more meaningful pause   full breath

X   end of thought   full breath, look at audience

XX   long pause   full breath, look at audience

XXX   longer pause   full breath, look at audience

Phrasing

"I'm proud to tell you this evening that your
ingenious and resourceful responses to the
problems created by the current industry-wide recession
have put the travelers at ease."
"We are painfully aware of the incredible challenges
you have faced in recent months and appreciate your
renewed efforts on our behalf."

Emphasis

This year that is drawing to a close undoubtedly will go
down as the words in the history of the casualty-property
business.

Other Symbols

    WARNING: Slide change coming.

    CUE: Change slide. Place in text exactly where slide
            change comes.

    louder

    softer

spaced version with all the markings. Both these versions are neat-margin versions. Notice how many bridges are necessary to indicate thoughts carried over to the next line.

Double-Spaced Version with Neat Margins

FOUR SCORE AND SEVEN YEARS AGO/OUR FATHERS BROUGHT/FORTH

UPON THIS CONTINENT/A NEW NATION/CONCEIVED IN LIBERTY,/AND

DEDICATED TO THE PROPOSITION/THAT ALL MEN ARE CREATED

EQUAL. XX

NOW WE ARE ENGAGED IN A GREAT CIVIL WAR,/TESTING WHETHER

THAT NATION,/OR ANY NATION/SO CONCEIVED/AND SO

DEDICATED,/CAN LONG ENDURE.XWE ARE MET ON A GREAT

BATTLEFIELD OF THAT WAR.XWE HAVE COME TO DEDICATE A PORTION

OF THAT FIELD/AS A FINAL RESTING-PLACE/FOR THOSE/WHO HERE

GAVE THEIR LIVES/THAT THAT NATION MIGHT LIVE.XIT IS ALTOGETHER

FITTING AND PROPER THAT WE SHOULD DO THIS. XX

BUT IN A LARGER SENSE/WE CANNOT DEDICATE,//WE CANNOT

CONSECRATE,/WE CANNOT HALLOW THIS GROUND.XTHE BRAVE

MEN,/LIVING AND DEAD,/WHO STRUGGLED HERE,/HAVE

CONSECRATED IT/FAR ABOVE OUR POOR POWER/TO ADD OR DETRACT. XX

THE WORLD WILL LITTLE NOTE,/NOR LONG REMEMBER,/WHAT WE

SAY HERE,XBUT IT CAN NEVER FORGET/WHAT THEY DID HERE.XIT IS

FOR US,/THE LIVING,/RATHER/TO BE DEDICATED HERE/TO THE

UNFINISHED WORK THEY HAVE/THUS FAR/SO NOBLY

ADVANCED.XIT IS RATHER FOR US/TO BE HERE DEDICATED TO THE

GREAT TASK/REMAINING BEFORE US THAT FROM/THESE HONOURED

DEAD/WE TAKE INCREASED DEVOTION/TO THAT CAUSE/FOR WHICH/

THEY HERE GAVE/THE LAST FULL MEASURE OF DEVOTION;THAT WE

HERE HIGHLY RESOLVE/THAT THE DEAD/SHALL NOT HAVE DIED IN

VAIN THAT THIS NATION, UNDER GOD,/SHALL HAVE A NEW BIRTH OF

FREEDOM;AND THAT GOVERNMENT/OF THE PEOPLE//BY THE

PEOPLE//AND FOR THE PEOPLE//SHALL NOT PERISH FROM THE EARTH. XXX

Triple-Spaced Version with Neat Margins

FOUR SCORE AND SEVEN YEARS AGO/OUR FATHERS BROUGHT/FORTH

UPON THIS CONTINENT/A NEW NATION/CONCEIVED IN LIBERTY,/AND

DEDICATED TO THE PROPOSITION/THAT ALL MEN ARE CREATED

EQUAL. X X

NOW WE ARE ENGAGED IN A GREAT CIVIL WAR,/TESTING WHETHER

THAT NATION,/OR ANY NATION/SO CONCEIVED/AND SO

DEDICATED,/CAN LONG ENDURE.X/WE ARE MET ON A GREAT

BATTLEFIELD OF THAT WAR.X/WE HAVE COME TO DEDICATE A PORTION

OF THAT FIELD/AS A FINAL RESTING-PLACE/FOR THOSE/WHO HERE

GAVE THEIR LIVES/THAT THAT NATION MIGHT LIVE.X/IT IS ALTOGETHER

FITTING AND PROPER THAT WE SHOULD DO THIS. X X

BUT IN A LARGER SENSE/WE CANNOT DEDICATE//WE CANNOT

CONSECRATE,/WE CANNOT HALLOW THIS GROUND.X/THE BRAVE

MEN,/LIVING AND DEAD,/WHO STRUGGLED HERE,/HAVE

CONSECRATED IT/FAR ABOVE OUR POOR POWER/TO ADD OR DETRACT.XX

THE WORLD WILL LITTLE NOTE, NOR LONG REMEMBER, WHAT WE

SAY HERE BUT IT CAN NEVER FORGET WHAT THEY DID HERE IT IS

FOR US, THE LIVING, RATHER TO BE DEDICATED HERE TO THE

UNFINISHED WORK THEY HAVE THUS FAR SO NOBLY

ADVANCED IT IS RATHER FOR US TO BE HERE DEDICATED TO THE

GREAT TASK REMAINING BEFORE US THAT FROM THESE HONOURED

DEAD WE TAKE INCREASED DEVOTION TO THAT CAUSE FOR WHICH

THEY HERE GAVE THE LAST FULL MEASURE OF DEVOTION; THAT WE

HERE HIGHLY RESOLVE THAT THE DEAD SHALL NOT HAVE DIED IN

VAIN THAT THIS NATION, UNDER GOD, SHALL HAVE A NEW BIRTH OF

FREEDOM; AND THAT GOVERNMENT OF THE PEOPLE BY THE

PEOPLE, AND FOR THE PEOPLE SHALL NOT PERISH FROM THE EARTH. X X X

Version without Bridging

In the following version, all thoughts are completed on one line. The script looks quite a bit neater because there are no bridging marks, and you can concentrate on emphasis, breathing, and pause marks.

FOUR SCORE AND SEVEN YEARS AGO / OUR FATHERS /

BROUGHT FORTH UPON THIS CONTINENT / A NEW NATION /

CONCEIVED IN LIBERTY, / AND DEDICATED TO THE PROPOSITION /

THAT ALL MEN ARE CREATED EQUAL. X X

NOW WE ARE ENGAGED IN A GREAT CIVIL WAR, / TESTING /

WHETHER THAT NATION, / OR ANY NATION / SO CONCEIVED / AND

SO DEDICATED, / CAN LONG ENDURE X WE ARE MET

ON A GREAT BATTLEFIELD OF THAT WAR. X

WE HAVE COME TO DEDICATE / A PORTION OF THAT FIELD /

AS A FINAL RESTING-PLACE / FOR THOSE WHO HERE

GAVE THEIR LIVES / THAT THAT NATION MIGHT LIVE. X

IT IS ALTOGETHER FITTING AND PROPER / THAT WE SHOULD DO THIS. X X

BUT IN A LARGER SENSE / WE CANNOT DEDICATE, /

WE CANNOT CONSECRATE, WE CANNOT HALLOW THIS GROUND. X

THE BRAVE MEN, LIVING AND DEAD, WHO STRUGGLED HERE,

HAVE CONSECRATED IT FAR ABOVE OUR POOR POWER TO ADD OR DETRACT. XX

THE WORLD WILL LITTLE NOTE, NOR LONG REMEMBER,

WHAT WE SAY HERE BUT IT CAN NEVER FORGET WHAT THEY DID HERE. X

IT IS FOR US, THE LIVING, RATHER TO BE DEDICATED HERE

TO THE UNFINISHED WORK THEY HAVE THUS FAR SO NOBLY ADVANCED. X

IT IS RATHER FOR US TO BE HERE DEDICATED TO THE GREAT TASK

REMAINING BEFORE US, THAT FROM THESE HONOURED DEAD

WE TAKE INCREASED DEVOTION TO THAT CAUSE FOR WHICH THEY HERE GAVE

THE LAST FULL MEASURE OF DEVOTION THAT WE HERE

HIGHLY RESOLVE THAT THE DEAD SHALL NOT HAVE DIED IN VAIN, X

THAT THIS NATION, UNDER GOD, SHALL HAVE A NEW BIRTH OF FREEDOM; X

AND THAT GOVERNMENT OF THE PEOPLE BY THE PEOPLE,

AND FOR THE PEOPLE, SHALL NOT PERISH FROM THE EARTH. XXX

Teleprompter Version

The teleprompter script is written on continuous sheets of paper. Even if the pages are separated, it is easy to read from because it is written thought by thought.

FOUR SCORE AND SEVEN YEARS AGO

OUR FATHERS

BROUGHT FORTH UPON THIS CONTINENT

A NEW NATION

CONCEIVED IN LIBERTY,

AND DEDICATED TO THE PROPOSITION THAT

ALL MEN ARE CREATED EQUAL. X

    NOW WE ARE ENGAGED IN A GREAT CIVIL WAR,

TESTING WHETHER THAT NATION,

OR ANY NATION

SO CONCEIVED AND SO DEDICATED,

CAN LONG ENDURE. X

    WE ARE MET ON A GREAT BATTLEFIELD OF THAT WAR. X

WE HAVE COME TO DEDICATE A PORTION OF THAT FIELD

AS A FINAL RESTING-PLACE

FOR THOSE

WHO HERE GAVE THEIR LIVES THAT

THAT NATION MIGHT LIVE. X

IT IS ALTOGETHER FITTING AND PROPER

THAT WE SHOULD DO THIS. X

BUT IN A LARGER SENSE

WE CANNOT DEDICATE,

WE CANNOT CONSECRATE,

WE CANNOT HALLOW THIS GROUND. X

THE BRAVE MEN,

LIVING AND DEAD,

WHO STRUGGLED HERE,

HAVE CONSECRATED IT

FAR ABOVE OUR POOR POWER

TO ADD OR DETRACT. X

THE WORLD WILL LITTLE NOTE,

NOR LONG REMEMBER,

WHAT WE SAY HERE,

BUT IT CAN NEVER FORGET

WHAT THEY DID HERE. X

IT IS FOR US,

THE LIVING, RATHER

TO BE DEDICATED HERE

TO THE UNFINISHED WORK

THEY HAVE

THUS FAR

SO NOBLY ADVANCED. X

IT IS RATHER FOR US TO BE HERE DEDICATED

TO THE GREAT TASK

REMAINING BEFORE US, X

THAT FROM

THESE HONOURED DEAD

WE TAKE INCREASED DEVOTION

TO THAT CAUSE

FOR WHICH

THEY HERE GAVE

THE LAST FULL MEASURE OF DEVOTION; X

   THAT WE HERE HIGHLY RESOLVE

THAT THE DEAD

SHALL NOT HAVE DIED IN VAIN,

THAT THIS NATION, /UNDER GOD, /

SHALL HAVE A NEW BIRTH OF FREEDOM;

AND

THAT GOVERNMENT

OF THE PEOPLE,

BY THE PEOPLE,

AND FOR THE PEOPLE,

SHALL NOT PERISH FROM THE EARTH. X X X

Capitals and Lowercase Version

Although tradition dictates all capital letters, some people believe (and some research shows) that it's easier to read words typed in capitals and lowercase because the words are more recognizable. Read the following version and see what you think.

Four score and seven years ago/ our fathers /

brought forth upon this continent/ a new nation /

conceived in liberty, /and dedicated to the proposition

that all men are created equal. ✗✗

Now we are engaged in a great civil war,/ testing

whether that nation,/or any nation/so conceived/and

so dedicated,/can long endure.✗We are met

on a great battlefield of that war.✗

We have come to dedicate/a portion of that field /

as a final resting-place/for those who here

gave their lives/that that nation might live. ✗

It is altogether fitting and proper/that we should do this. ✗✗

But in a larger sense/we cannot dedicate, /

we cannot consecrate,/we cannot hallow this ground. ✗

The brave men,/living and dead,/who struggled here,

have consecrated it/far above our poor power/to add or detract. ✗✗

The world will little note,/nor long remember,

what we say here,✗but it can never forget what they did here. ✗

It is for us, the living, rather to be dedicated here

to the unfinished work they have thus far so nobly advanced. X

It is rather for us to be here dedicated to the great task

remaining before us that from these honoured dead /

we take increased devotion to that cause for which they here gave /

the last full measure of devotion that we here

highly resolve that the dead shall not have died in vain, X

that this nation, under God, shall have a new birth of freedom; X

and that government of the people by the people, //

and for the people shall not perish from the earth. X X X

Unmarked Script

Because your speaking style may not agree with mine, and because you may breathe using a different rhythm, I've given you an unmarked script to work on. Type it in the way that seems easiest first, either double- or triple-spaced, and either with a complete thought on one line or in teleprompter style. Then as you read, put in breath marks and pause marks. You might end by retyping it and remarking it once you've practiced several times. But you'll have a script from which you can easily read with style and elegance.

FOUR SCORE AND SEVEN YEARS AGO OUR FATHERS BROUGHT FORTH

UPON THIS CONTINENT A NEW NATION CONCEIVED IN LIBERTY, AND

DEDICATED TO THE PROPOSITION THAT ALL MEN ARE CREATED EQUAL.

NOW WE ARE ENGAGED IN A GREAT CIVIL WAR, TESTING WHETHER

THAT NATION, OR ANY NATION SO CONCEIVED AND SO DEDICATED, CAN

LONG ENDURE. WE ARE MET ON A GREAT BATTLEFIELD OF THAT WAR.

WE HAVE COME TO DEDICATE A PORTION OF THAT FIELD AS A FINAL

RESTINGPLACE FOR THOSE WHO HERE GAVE THEIR LIVES THAT THAT

NATION MIGHT LIVE. IT IS ALTOGETHER FITTING AND PROPER THAT WE

SHOULD DO THIS.

BUT IN A LARGER SENSE WE CANNOT DEDICATE, WE CANNOT

CONSECRATE, WE CANNOT HALLOW THIS GROUND. THE BRAVE MEN,

LIVING AND DEAD, WHO STRUGGLED HERE, HAVE CONSECRATED IT FAR

ABOVE OUR POOR POWER TO ADD OR DETRACT.

THE WORLD WILL LITTLE NOTE, NOR LONG REMEMBER, WHAT WE

SAY HERE, BUT IT CAN NEVER FORGET WHAT THEY DID HERE. IT IS FOR

US, THE LIVING, RATHER TO BE DEDICATED HERE TO THE UNFINISHED

WORK THEY HAVE THUS FAR SO NOBLY ADVANCED. IT IS RATHER FOR

US TO BE HERE DEDICATED TO THE GREAT TASK REMAINING BEFORE US,

THAT FROM THESE HONOURED DEAD WE TAKE INCREASED DEVOTION TO

THAT CAUSE FOR WHICH THEY HERE GAVE THE LAST FULL MEASURE OF

DEVOTION; THAT WE HERE HIGHLY RESOLVE THAT THE DEAD SHALL

NOT HAVE DIED IN VAIN, THAT THIS NATION, UNDER GOD, SHALL HAVE

A NEW BIRTH OF FREEDOM; AND THAT GOVERNMENT OF THE PEOPLE,

BY THE PEOPLE, AND FOR THE PEOPLE, SHALL NOT PERISH FROM THE

EARTH.

12

HOW TO ANSWER QUESTIONS

The way to pick up loose ends is in the question and answer period. A few simple techniques will help you clarify, explain, recommend, or reassure after you've taken a position.

One of the frustrations of presentation is not having sufficient time to cover the topic adequately. When you are given forty-five minutes to cover a topic that needs four hours, you wonder, "Am I giving people the information they need? Am I making myself clear? Do they understand me?" The question and answer period will go a long way toward picking up those loose ends. That's why you must always make allowances for a question and answer period. A rule of thumb is 15 to 20 percent of your allotted time.

It could be that you have been invited as an expert, part of someone else's presentation. Maybe you are the securities expert who will answer technical questions about the school board's proposal for a new bond issue. Or perhaps you're the doctor expected to calm parents' panic about the flu epidemic.

Here's how you handle the question and answer period.

DO YOUR HOMEWORK!

You can't anticipate every situation, but try. Bone up on the field. Read the pertinent books. Part of your homework must include staying abreast of current events. Read all the local newspapers. Read the trade and professional press. It could be very embarassing to find out from someone in the audience that the person you've been praising so highly is suing your company or that one of the homes you just built has been condemned.

SET YOUR OWN AGENDA

Set your own rules for fielding questions and state them up front. Will you accept questions anytime, or do you want your audience to save them for the end?

PRIME THE PUMP

Most people are reluctant to be the first one to ask a question. If you want to stimulate questions, plant someone in the audience to ask the first question. Failing that, if you see someone who looks like he or she has a question, ask, ''Do you have a question, Sir?'' or ''Do you have a question, Jane?'' If you know that person's name, it's preferable to use it. The more you personalize your presentation, the better. As usual, you must exercise good judgment and diplomacy.

LISTEN TO THE QUESTION

Never let your guard down. Stay alert. Concentrate on your questioner ''eyeball to eyeball.'' Don't forget, you listen best with your eyes. When it's appropriate, smile a lot. Smiling or not, always project concern and warmth. Love the person to whom you're listening and answering.

Being ready means being concentrated.
—John Strasberg, quoted in *The New Generation of Acting Teachers*

Never cross your arms while listening; when you do this you are projecting a negative and defensive stance. It's best to let your arms dangle loosely by your side or to rest your fingertips lightly on the podium. This is the only circumstance in which you may touch the podium. If you're sitting, let your arms rest in a relaxed manner on the arms of your chair or on your lap. Don't clench your fists.

Don't fidget with a pencil, cigarette lighter, or papers. Don't doodle on your yellow pad. And don't smoke. The way you puff can reveal inner turmoil.

SHOW RESPECT FOR THE QUESTIONER

No matter how much you disapprove of a person's appearance or manner of speech, don't show it. Be courteous to all,

---

This chapter and the next are greatly interrelated. However, I've written them separately because your answers serve different purposes. In this chapter, the answers are designed to clarify, explain, recommend, or reassure after you've taken a position. In Chapter 13, besides doing all the above, the answers may also serve to advertise, promote, reverse or defuse either a negative situation or an impression created by someone else. So if some of the recommended techniques seem repetitious, bear in mind that they serve different purposes.

regardless of their wardrobe, hairstyle, accent, gender, or ethnic background. Also, to paraphrase Shakespeare, neither an obsequious twit nor a wise guy be. Don't kowtow to rank or act superior to your questioner, and, for heaven's sake, don't talk down. Be your courteous, diplomatic, tactful best.

NET OUT YOUR ANSWER

Listen carefully to the question. Nod to signify you're following and understand the question. Unless absolutely necessary, don't interrupt. Occasionally, you might decide to interrupt because a person is making a false assumption or a derogatory statement. Even in this instance, it might be better to wait until the end of the question and then set that person right.

Try not to begin your answer until the entire question has been asked. Perhaps you're a teacher or a consultant who's in demand, and you've made the same presentation many times. You have been asked the same question over and over, and you are primed with an answer. It is good practice to behave as if no one ever asked that question before. Pause as if framing your answer . . . and deliver the answer you've prefabricated.

Learn to structure your response like this:

1. Give your point of view or recommendation.
2. Explain how you arrived at that conclusion.

Remember at all times that you are a salesperson, that you are a missionary, that you must sell your point of view.

Don't ramble. Keep your answers short but complete.

Net it out! Give specific examples. Don't talk about fruit; talk about kiwis and kumquats. Use analogies. They help clarify, just like showing a picture of your trophy moose enhances your description.

Answer only the question asked. Don't volunteer information that's not pertinent, especially if it's negative or if the other person has no need to know.

LEARN HOW TO TAME THE GADFLY

You don't have to answer unfair or nonrelevant questions. For instance:

Gadfly: "Have you stopped beating your spouse?"
You: "I never, ever beat my spouse. The issue that concerns us is . . . ."
         Or
         "I cannot answer that question with a simple yes or no. I never, ever abused my spouse. The issue that concerns us is . . . ."

Questions that seek information you think is inappropriate or that you will cover later, or questions that are complex can be answered as follows:

You: "An explanation of our accounting practices is outside the realm of today's discussion. If you'll address your question to our accountant, Joe Blackink, I'm sure he'd be glad to . . . ."
         Or
         "We are going to cover that topic fully in our next segment."
         Or
         "You have really asked me four questions. Let's address them one at a time."

Don't let one person dominate the question period. Tell that person, "I'd like to give some others a chance to ask questions. If you'll meet me right after the meeting, I'll be happy to address the rest of your questions." Or refer the questioner to the proper authority. Be firm but polite.

NEVER LET YOURSELF GET ANGRY!

"All well and good," you say, "But suppose that gadfly, that smart aleck, makes a remark that makes me angry?"

You must never, never allow yourself the luxury of getting angry. Many a promising career has been cut short by anger, by the coarse put-down, by the bigoted one-liner. Anger is particularly fatal to people in public life.

Shoot not from the hip. If you shoot from the hip, you usually shoot yourself in the foot. And that's not easy because your foot will be in your mouth. An off-hand wisecrack or putdown can be tomorrow's headline out of context.

Now anyone can get angry—we are, after all, human. How do you prevent yourself from making an angry response?

It ain't easy, but it can be done. It all begins with your attitude going in. "A soft answer turneth away wrath," according to Proverbs. I recommend that you lavish your tormentor with all the love you can muster. The Bible says, "Love thy enemies." Love is the greatest strength you have to counter hostility.

Love? Yes, love.

Love and patience are the great temper defusers. Here we get back to Psychology 101. How can someone be nasty to a person who loves them? Someone can end up only appreciating your good judgment.

So Mr. Tormenter shoots you a zinger. A whipcrack response is the worst one you can give. The more outrage you feel, the slower, more deliberate, and more friendly you must become. Before you say word one, take a nice, leisurely, deep breath. Count one thousand, two thousand, three thousand. Then answer.

If the pressure gets really hot, speak—in fact, do everything in slo w m o t i o n.

It'll come out just right.

President Ronald Reagan handled all the above by injecting the word *well* before his answers. That one little device gave him the time to frame his answer in a suitable manner.

AVOID TRANQUILIZERS OR ALCOHOL

One of the worst things you can do to yourself is to use alcohol or tranquilizers before your presentation to fight stage fright.

These artificial means of inducing calmness lessen your powers of self-control. You can make a fool of yourself and you won't be aware that you're doing it. Your speech can get fuzzy. You can lose your train of thought. I've seen it happen to some very brilliant people—people in the top echelons earning six-figure salaries.

Don't do it to yourself. See "Use First Aid for Muscular Tension" in Chapter 8.

KILL THAT CLICHE

Avoid corny phrases like "I'm glad you asked that question" or "That's a good question." Too many people equate that kind of statement with stalling for time while you think of a good answer.

WOULD YOU REPEAT THAT?

There are several schools of thought on whether to repeat the question. Some recommend that you repeat every question. I am not of that school. If everyone in the room has heard the question, it becomes redundant to repeat it.

Repeat the question in the following situations:

- The questioner mumbles or is otherwise inaudible.
- The questioner in the front of the room can't be heard by the people in the back.
- You want to stall for time while you formulate your answer.

When you don't understand the question, say "I don't understand the question. Would you please repeat it?"

PART FOUR

USING THE METHOD TO PERFORM LIKE A PRO IN OTHER SITUATIONS

13

HOW TO MEET THE MEDIA

When you're meeting the media either by their choice or yours, doing your homework, anticipating possible questions, practicing, and dressing appropriately help you to be your best, most responsive self.

All requests for you to perform are not equal. Even though you might be a seasoned presenter, three occasions can strike even greater terror in your heart:

1. Appearing before an income tax auditor.
2. Participating in your own wedding ceremony.
3. Being interviewed on television.

For the first, see your accountant. For the second, consult your clergy person. For the third, read this chapter. In all three intances, my original admonition to be yourself is the best advice I can give you.

The guidelines in Chapter 12 on how to conduct a question-and-answer period also pertain to media interviews.

There are two general categories of media to discuss: print and broadcast. I will principally discuss the television and radio interview. However, a great deal of what applies to performance in front of the camera or on the air applies as well to being interviewed by a newspaper or magazine reporter.

Interviews for whatever medium fall into two basic categories: when you are invited to appear and when you asked to be invited.

WHEN YOU ARE INVITED

If you're invited to appear for an interview, someone in the editorial department senses that you have done something newsworthy or can supply information that is newsworthy. Your appearance may concern you personally, your company or industry, your political party, or your profession.

There is no cause for panic. Reporters are basically nice, decent, honest people. But you must remember this, from the lowly cub to the superstar, they have a job to do. They've got to deliver interesting copy for their audience. They are always on the lookout for the new, the different, the exciting. When a dog bites a man, that's not news. When a man bites a dog, *that's* news.

Do Your Homework

Why Did They Invite *You*?

An an interviewee, you have the right (and you should exercise it) to find out why you were invited and not someone else. What information do you have that your interviewer is interested in? Will there be a panel discussion? If so, who are the other panelists? What are their affiliations? Are their beliefs the same as yours, or are you providing an opposing viewpoint?

Approximately how much air time will you get? If the interviewer can be specific, know your parameters. If it sounds like the interviewer is on a fishing expedition, you've got a heck of a lot more research to do.

Listen to the Show

If there's time, listen to the show. It's a good idea to be familiar with the format and the interviewer's style. Will you have a block of time in which to present your information? Or will the interviewer intersperse comments and questions? Does the interviewer ask in-depth questions for which you'll need to know a lot of details? Or does the interviewer expect broad, sweeping answers with few details?

Steep Yourself in Information

Read every newspaper you can get your hands on. Be sure to read your trade or professional publications, both current and back issues. Find out if there's something in them about you, your company, your industry, or your area of expertise. If there is, that will give you a clue about what to bone up on.

Don't skip a day. Don't miss the weekend editions. A lot of vital information appears in the Saturday and Sunday editions. Be especially sure to read the press the day of the telecast. It's embarassing, to say the least, to be informed on the air that your restaurant has just been fined for unsanitary conditions.

Anticipate Pertinent Questions

Try to anticipate the questions you'll be asked. Once you know why you have been invited and you've loaded yourself with information, you should be able to list some pertinent questions you might be asked. Jotting them down as they occur to you is important because it helps you see categories. Do you think the interviewer is primarily after facts about your industry or your particular job? Is there false information you'll have to set straight? Will you be expected to state your view about a current controversy?

In preparing your answers, remember to structure them so the most important part of what you have to say is most likely to be heard.

There Are Two Basic Ways of Telling a Story

If you attempt, up front, to explain how you arrived at your conclusion, the information you want your viewers to know—your message—may never reach the audience. It is journalistic practice to chop off from the bottom of the story arbitrarily to fit a time slot or space. So your side of the story could very well end up on the cutting-room floor if you talk first about how you got on that side of the story.

Telling it the way it occurred—beginning, middle, end—is called the pyramidal structure. Journalistic structure uses the inverted pyramid. It begins with what happened—including who, when, and where—and follows with why it happened.

A story written using the pyramidal structure goes something like this:

> Gregg Yuppee had a very aggravating day at the office. That night he couldn't sleep. He tossed and he turned and he looked at the ceiling. As a result, he got out of bed the next morning grouchy, grouchy, grouchy. His wife, Yolanda, fixed him his usual breakfast of corn flakes and hot water with a cup of coffee. Gregg found fault with everything. The corn flakes were too hard. The water too tepid. The coffee too weak. Yolanda, who by that time had had it up to here, answered in kind. Pretty soon they were in a rip-roaring argument during which she listed his 3,000 inadequacies. That did it! He pushed away his flakes, grabbed his attaché case, and slammed out the door. Crossing the street to the bus stop, he was struck by a garbage truck and killed.

That's the way it happened. It takes a long time to get to the point of the story—that Gregg Yuppee was killed in an accident.

The news media would tell the same story as follows:

EXECUTIVE KILLED BY TRUCK

> Gregg Yuppee, president of Terrific Trivia Corporation, was knocked over and killed by a garbage truck while crossing Broadway at 7:30 this morning.

Then the writer would go into the events that led up to the accident.

In formulating your answers, the inverted pyramid is the most effective. If you can answer with a headline—great! I said it in Chapter 12, and I'm repeating it here because it's so important: net out your answer. Let your answer start with your bottom-line message.

A pyramidal or sequential response would go something like this: "Because of the recent measles epidemic, the hospital is overcrowded. It is a potentially dangerous situation for both patients and staff. That's why we are proud to announce that we are building an ultramodern, 800-bed annex."

If you answer that way, when your statement is edited, you're likely to hear yourself saying the following: "Because of the recent measles epidemic, the hospital is overcrowded. It is a potentially dangerous situation for both patients and staff." The new wing isn't mentioned.

If you use the inverted pyramid, your answer should sound something like this: "We are proud to announce that we are planning to build an ultramodern, 800-bed annex. We were alerted to the need because of the potentially dangerous situation for patients and staff due to overcrowding during the recent measles epidemic."

Keep Alert

Your good reporter will realize that you've read this book and that you are on the lookout for traps. Before the show, he or she might try to get you off your guard, hoping you'll reveal a juicy nugget. You may get the buddy-buddy treatment. That very often works. It's heady stuff to have Harry Superscoop rest his hand on your shoulder and call you by name.

The reporter might even let you buy him or her a drink. (A reporter seldom buys anything.) Or you might get the old "Well now that the interview is over. . . ." treatment. The reporter is searching for an angle and hopes that, with your guard down, you might just let slip something you don't want revealed. So keep alert.

Nothing Is Ever off the Record

Concentrate on your interviewer . . . eyeball to eyeball.
Never lose sight of why you're there. Concentrate on your
objective, your mission.

Nothing is ever off the record to a good reporter. Never
say in the restroom what you wouldn't and shouldn't say in
front of the camera.

At the same time, you must bear in mind that reporters
are not evil people. They are just doing their job. They are
not the enemy. In fact, they can often become that friend
in need when you want to get information to an audience.

> *Be aware of the objective as the target of your action—I am going there. I know I am going there.*
> —Morris Carnovsky, quoted in *Actors Talk about Acting*

You Have Rights

You have the right not to answer a question that is misleading
or irrelevant to your message. If your interviewer asks such
a question, don't ignore it. Point out that it is misleading or
irrelevant and segue into an answer to the question you wish
had been asked so you can tell the audience what you want
it to know. (Segue, pronounced seg-way, is a musical term
meaning to make a smooth transition from one theme to
another.)

For instance, "The fact that I am getting divorced is not
what should concern us here. Of great momentary concern
is that we must raise six million dollars to build the new
children's wing at the hospital, and we could accomplish that
if . . . ."

What if the interviewer bases a question on a false
premise, such as "How does your company plan to dispose
of the pollutants you now dump into Lake Goober?" You
answer, "We've never polluted that lake. We have the most
modern equipment to dispose of pollutants." (Here comes
the segue.) "And when we get the variance to build the extension of our plant, we will install the same state-of-the-art
equipment that we've employed all these years."

Sometimes a reporter will ask a question based on a false
premise and demand a yes or no answer. If either answer

will lead to a false impression like that old chestnut, "Have you stopped beating your spouse?" you say, "I never, ever beat my spouse. (Segue) In tomorrow's meeting, the City Council will discuss whether to grant a variance in the Bushwick area so our company can expand its facilities. If the council votes yes, that will mean at least a thousand new jobs for our townspeople." Whenever possible, point out the benefit to society.

And remember, stay away from acronyms and technical or insider jargon. Stay away from clichés like "I'm glad you asked that question" or "That's a good question."

WHEN YOU WANT TO BE INVITED

If a radio or television appearance would be advantageous for you to solicit funds or plug a product, service, book, or lecture, here's how to go about getting an invitation to be interviewed:

- Phone the station and ask the name of the producer.
- Write the producer a letter telling what is interesting or unusual about you, your product, or your program.
- Follow up in a few days with a phone call to the producer. If at first you don't succeed, try, try, try again.

PRACTICE, BABY, PRACTICE!

Whether you were invited or got yourself invited, you must practice your answers out loud. Sure, you must anticipate the questions, and, sure, you must work out your answers, but if you don't hear yourself say them out loud, they may not come out as planned when you're in the crunch. You may find yourself injecting spontaneous and, too often, detrimental statements.

Write down the anticipated questions. (You've heard this before—write it down.)

Involve your public relations counselor if you have one. If you don't have a public relations counselor, practice with someone from the company. Let this person read the questions while you practice being the guest. Ask for a critique of your answers. It's a good idea to record the session on a cassette so you'll hear yourself as others will hear you.

If you can't get either kind of help, trot out our old friend the cassette and record your responses. You'll be able to critique your answers more objectively. In evaluating your performance, remember that most people in the audience are not experts. Favor them. Will the lay person understand?

IT'S SHOW TIME!

How should you dress? When selecting your clothes for the telecast, the word for both men and women is *conservative*. Solid colors in suits, shirts, dresses, skirts, and blouses are best. Women should stay away from reds, oranges, or yellows. Also stay away from large prints or plaids. Men's ties should be dark with very little pattern. Men's socks should be solid and kneelength. Don't wear distracting jewelry. No diamond tiepin. No glittering earrings. If you must wear jewelry, make it unobtrusive.

Be punctual. You'll be instructed when to show up by the production staff. Be on time or be earlier.

Ask the producer about makeup. Your exceedingly high forehead might need some toning down to avoid reflecting lights. Women should have their makeup checked by the production staff. Minimal makeup for all is good advice.

Anticipate delays. During tapings of the show, especially, there can be many delays and interruptions. Be patient, and don't get revved up too soon. A camera may go down, or a floodlight may pop. Your star interviewer may not be satisfied with his or her performance and want another take. If you're getting edgy, deep breathing will help you keep calm. So will a conversation with another person.

Before taking your place on the set, neaten up. Comb your hair, button your jacket, check your fly, etc. Once seated, sit tall but relaxed. Do not slump in the chair. If you love yourself, don't fidget.

What should you do with your hands? When listening,

let your hands and forearms rest loosely on your lap or the arms of the chair. Do not clasp your hands. In fact, don't touch hand to hand ever. When speaking, as advised in the chapter on performance skills, talk with your hands.

To project sincerity and intimacy, establish an eyeball-to-eyeball relationship with two people and switch your attention between them. The first person is your interviewer. The other person is the camera with the red light on. Treat the camera lens as you would a set of eyes. Actually, the lens *is* a set of eyes because what the lens sees, the audience sees.

Keep your answers short—short but not rushed. Your time on a nightly newscast could be from thirty to ninety seconds. On a news special, an interviewer could devote as much as ten minutes to your segment. Ten seconds is a long time. So is thirty seconds. Most television commercials are thirty seconds long, and they succeed in grabbing your attention, interesting you in their product, and asking you to buy.

If you want to find out how much you can say in a brief time, try this. Set a timer to thirty seconds. Read from a newspaper until the bell rings. You'll be amazed how much you can say in that time. Try the same with ten seconds and sixty seconds. Of course, you must bear in mind that there will be two of you speaking—you and the interviewer. So the more concise you are, the more time you'll have to express your viewpoint.

Speak conversationally, the way you would to your dearest chum. And, for heaven's sake, under all circumstances, *lo-o-o-ve* your interviewer!

14

HOW TO USE THE TELEPHONE TO YOUR ADVANTAGE

Learn how to use radio techniques to sell yourself on the telephone.

Eighty-five percent of your work day is spent communicating. A lion's share of this communicating is done on the telephone:

- Making appointments
- Gathering information
- Ordering
- Requisitioning
- Keeping in touch
- Selling
- Soliciting
- Complaining
- Answering complaints

More presentations are made on the telephone than through all other media except radio and television.

KEEP COLD CALLS WARM

Telephone communication has several advantages. It's convenient; you don't even have to leave your office. It's relatively inexpensive, and it's quick. Plus you get an immediate response.

However, telephone communication has one great disadvantage—the person you're talking with cannot see you. He or she can't see how good-looking you are, how expensively dressed, how animated. You are limited to your voice quality and your warmth and wit to make a positive impression.

Telephone solicitation has become a fact of life. People use the telephone in selling anything from magazine subscriptions to real estate to tickets to the police officers' ball. Some of these callers you immediately hang up on. Some callers you listen to for awhile even if you don't buy. Some callers you actually buy from, or contribute to, or volunteer to help.

Haven't you found that the warmer, the friendlier, the more natural the voice, the more you pay attention?

Stay away from the back-slapping heartiness of the snake oil salesman. You know—the "I'll tell ya what I'm gonna do" approach. I have a friend who has a good response to this kind of situation. When a hearty voice says, "Hi! I'm Mike with the Swamp Land Company! How are you today?!!" my friend answers, "I'm fine" and hangs up.

USE RADIO PERFORMANCE TECHNIQUES

Radio is another instance of communicating when you are deprived of visual impressions. Yet people are motivated to buy billions of dollars worth of products and services by the voice of the announcer or disc jockey alone. Although you can't see the radio personality, she or he is using all the techniques in the performance skills flow chart in Chapter 7.

If you ever witnessed a radio broadcast, the announcer doesn't just sit at the table placidly talking or reading the commercials. She or he is a bundle of energy, talking intimately with animation and affection into the microphone.

Here's how to present/communicate by telephone:

1. Consider the phone itself as your audience.
2. Psych yourself up to performance pitch.

3. Place the telephone mouthpiece no more than an inch and a half from your mouth.
4. Speak as if you are having an intimate conversation with your closest friend.
5. Pretend your closest friend is hard of hearing.
6. Establish eye contact with the cradle of your telephone. This may sound exotic, but it does influence how warm and friendly your voice sounds. One of my pupils who did telephone solicitation all day long cut the eye portion of a beautiful model from a magazine and pasted it on his phone. While he talked, he maintained eye contact. You don't really have to go that far, but if it helps, go ahead.
7. Smile at the telephone. The phone company talks about "the voice with the smile." When you smile as you talk, your voice will sound very friendly and warm.
8. Don't slouch. Sit comfortably upright. Gesture naturally with your free hand. This will lend excitement and magnetism to your voice.
9. Remember, your voice reflects how you feel. When you feel yourself flagging, take a short break. (See "What to Do at the Poop-out Point" below.)

USE THE KEY WORDS TO SELL BY PHONE

You'd probably tell me you'd as much consider winging a face-to-face sales presentation as you would consider climbing Mount Everest. Nevertheless, I'll bet you wing many a phone presentation. Don't. After about an hour on the phone, you are likely to begin to leave out key sales points.

A method used by many radio announcers can be of great use to you if you use the phone to sell, solicit, take surveys, or find a job. On the radio, the commercial is very often written out to be read verbatim by the announcer. However, a written presentation isn't flexible enough for the give and take of telephone communication. The preferred method is to list the main sales points.

Listing gives you much more flexibility. Listing is effec-

tive whether you are soliciting for a single item like a charitable fund, or whether you have a number of products like
stocks and bonds, real estate, or insurance.

Prepare a separate, tabbed fact sheet for each product
or issue, listing its selling points, facts, figures, and other
pertinent information ordered from most important to least
important. Enclose the fact sheets in a loose-leaf binder so
they won't get lost.

"You're interested in bonds?" Flip to the bond pages.

It will be helpful, if you are working with different products, to use different-colored paper for different products.

The above guidelines will also be very helpful when you conduct a teleconference. Set your agenda as you would in a face-to-face meeting, but list on a separate sheet each item on the agenda and the points you want to cover under that item.

WHAT TO DO AT THE POOP-OUT POINT

Constantly speaking and/or selling by phone is the most ener-vating of any form of presentation. Somewhere during the day you are going to feel lower than a snake's belly. You will feel exhausted, or negative, or discouraged, or cranky, or cross, or depressed, or all of the above.

You have reached the "poop-out point."

Don't proceed. Since your voice reflects your mood, it would be counterproductive to proceed. No matter how far you are from achieving your quota, take a break, a seventh-inning stretch. Go wash your face. Meditate. Read the fun-nies. You can do isometrics, but it's better to get up and walk a little.

While on the phone, soothe your throat. Have a cup of tea or coffee. Have a glass of juice. Something sweet and syrupy will lubricate your throat and give you a quick energy lift. My mother always said to drink pear juice or apricot nectar. I know she was never wrong because she told me so, and mothers never lie.

Never but *never* drink anything alcoholic while working.

If you must answer the phone while you're feeling negative, do this. Before you pick up the receiver, take two or three very deep breaths. Then pick up the phone and talk as if you were talking to your sweetheart!

WHERE DO WE GO FROM HERE?

If you don't do it,
it won't work.

A few years ago I bought my wife an exercise bicycle. It was a beauty, the top of the line, equipped with bells and timers and mileage indicators. And you could adjust it to peddle uphill or down. My wife loved it. But it sits in a corner of our bedroom with only ten miles on it. I'm thinking of using it as a planter. Or perhaps a place to hang my clothes overnight.

READING IS NOT ENOUGH

Buying and reading this how-to book isn't enough to acquire the skills to fully be yourself and tell 'em whatcha wanna tell 'em.

Motivational speaking is highly physical. Just as my wife's muscle tone was not improved by the mere possession of her exercise equipment, your speaking skills will not improve unless you religiously employ the required exercises I've suggested.

Bear in mind that I've designed this book as a practical instrument to be used by busy people. You can sandwich the exercises into your already crowded schedule. Do some while taking a shower, mowing the lawn, driving your car, or washing the dishes. Or take a few minutes before or after lunch. Of course, a regularly designated time slot is best.

EXERCISE!

If you don't use a tool, it rusts. Unless you exercise your communication muscles, they will atrophy. You just cannot wish a physical skill into existence. Knowing what's needed is not enough. If it were, the world would be full of great golfers and superb tennis players.

If you want to be a great speaker, you must practice speaking. You must render yourself articulate. You must get used to the sound of your voice. People cannot hear what you're saying inside; they must hear *you*.

Your best bet is to make as many actual presentations as you can. Failing that, tell jokes and anecdotes. Discuss politics, religion, and sports. Teach a Sunday school class, but act out the Bible stories, don't just read them. If you have young children, act out the bedtime stories. Join an amateur theatre group or a choir.

Take a class in aerobics—any kind of dancing is great! Any activity that encourages you to express yourself physically and energize yourself will help you to develop your communication skills. An especially good way to improve your give-and-take verbal skills is to play the game of charades. Acting out the name of a song or movie against a time limit really sharpens your communication capabilities.

PROMOTE YOURSELF

To get to the top of the ladder, most of the time you have to furnish your own ladder. Being a speaker who talks simply, powerfully, and naturally is one of the most effective ladders for career advancement.

That is, if you know what you're talking about. You must have substance. You must do your homework. The bubble soon bursts for the hot-air artist, for the person whose only skill is patting himself or herself on the back. No matter how attractively hot air is packaged, it is still hot air (as too many of our elected politicians are proving).

The effective speaker gets picked for the better assignments, so don't hide your light under a bushel. When your name comes up at a meeting, everyone there should know exactly what you look like and nod approval. If you automatically head for the back seat in the room, you're in for a life of obscurity.

As a young man, my sister's brother-in-law, Al, joined a large pencil company as sales promotion manager. The firm employed at least a dozen top-flight salesmen, and Al used to liven up the staff meetings by telling funny stories. Pretty soon, management tapped him as a principal speaker at sales meetings, distribution meetings, industrial seminars, and conventions. His prominence led to a very lucrative job offer from another company and eventually to his becoming president of a leading office products manufacturer.

YOU KNOW THE METHOD

You might ask, "How long do I have to continue this exercise program?"

My answer depends on your professionalism.

You see, the true professional forever seeks ways to upgrade a performance. Several years ago, I watched Barbara Walters interview the late Sir Laurence Olivier. He was then well into his eighties and considered the world's greatest living actor by people in the profession. He told her in essence that after every performance he asked himself, "How can I improve my next performance?"

In the heart of the theatre district in New York City, a former church houses an actors' workshop that offers classes to stars the caliber of Dustin Hoffman, Paul Newman, Shelley Winters, and Joanne Woodward. Great dancers like Mikhail Baryshnikov attend dance classes.

Professional ball players like Magic Johnson, Nolan Ryan, and Joe Montana show up for preseason training. Doctors and lawyers also attend seminars. (I don't know about Indian chiefs.) Most great corporations maintain full-time training departments to refresh and upgrade the skills of even their highest executives.

USE IT!

A true professional is never finished.

You've read this book. You know the method. You know how to say *what you want to say, the way you want to say it, at the time you want to say it.*

There's an old, old story of one man stopping another on a street in New York City. "Sir," he asked, "how do you get to Carnegie Hall?" The other replied, "Practice, man! Practice!"

So if you want to get to the top of the heap as a speaker, *practice!!!!*

This is a true story . . . my next-door neighbor, Cynthia, is an avid golfer. One day as she was teeing off . . . .

THE ULTIMATE EXERCISES— TWENTY-ONE FUNNY STORIES FOR PRACTICE

THE HOW AND WHY OF STORYTELLING

For self-instruction in the skills of presentation, there is no better medium for practicing performance skills than telling a joke.

It stands to reason that if you try to inflict your presentation, no matter how brilliant, on your friends and relatives at a luncheon, party, or picnic, you'll find yourself the world's prize room-emptier. However, by telling a funny story you will keep their interest and develop the necessary speaking skills.

Jokes are such a good medium because they are a microcosm of two very good art forms that depend on performance skills: plays and television commercials.

Jokes and plays have these elements in common: the setup, the crisis, and the payoff. *Hamlet, Pygmalion,* and *South Pacific* have the same construction. This structure can be compared to a television commercial, in which the elements are called the grabber, the rationale, and the call for action (you want the audience to laugh, buy, or applaud).

In telling a joke effectively, you must use all the disciplines that make a good broadcast commercial plus all the skills necessary to perform in a play.

Jokes are a form of folktale. I've heard the stories in this collection all over the United States and in many European countries where I've taught. I selected them for their actability and for their acceptability in mixed company.

Please don't memorize. Familiarize yourself with the gist of the story, and tell it in your own words. For best results, personalize and localize your joke. Tell it about yourself, your family, or mutual acquaintances, using your locality or business. If you are adept at accents, that's yet another enhancement. Be careful, however, that your dialect is not offensive.

PRACTICE STORIES

It was 5:30 p.m. in the darkest jungle in darkest Africa, and Tarzan, the ape man, had put in a tiring day doing whatever it is that ape men do. He was ready to go back to his little grass shack where his wife, Jane, and his son, Boy, were waiting.

As he was walking, there in front of him were these two giant water buffalo blocking his path. They charged him. In five minutes he had killed them both, and he continued on his way. Not a halfmile up the path, two humungous boa constrictors dropped down on him. Pulling out his trusty dagger, he had them sliced up like so much bologna in a trice. Undaunted, he went whistling down the trail only to be confronted by five furious bull elephants. It took no more than eight minutes, and he had them on their backs, their feet bound and their trunks braided.

By that time, he had reached the lagoon, on the other side of which was his home. Before he could dive into the water, eight alligators surrounded him, wanting him for their dinner. Out came his trusty dagger—swish, swish, stab, stab, cut, cut—and only the makings of thirty-five alligator purses were left. He dived into the water and was swimming in the middle of the lake when he was attacked by 400,000 piranhas. By the time Tarzan was through, the lake was full of piranha-burger meat.

Tarzan swam the last few yards, dragged himself up the ladder to his living room, and plopped himself into his favorite armchair panting with exhaustion. In came lovely Jane from the kitchen, gave him a great big smooch, and asked how his day had been. Tarzan just lay there, panting. He said one word, "Martini!"

Jane was astonished. "Tarzan, you?"

"Martini!" he repeated (pant, pant). "Extra dry. No olive."

Jane was upset, but she gave him one.

He chug-a-lugged it and handed her the glass. (Pant. Pant.) "Another martini."

After the third martini, she was distraught. "Tarzan, baby, what's wrong?"

He slouched there, panting. "Jane, you don't know the half of it. It's a jungle out there!"

Over the Pearly Gates in Heaven, there were two signs. One of them read, "For men who have always been dominated by their wives." That line extended for miles, as far as the eye could see. The other sign read, "For men who were never dominated by their wives." Under that sign was one timid-looking little man.

St. Peter surveyed the first long line and then walked over to the little man and asked, "Why are you the only one standing here?"

The man answered, "Beats me. My wife told me to stand here."

A pilot crashed in the middle of the Mohave Desert. He was unhurt and started to walk in what he thought was a westerly direction. It was very hot and he was very thirsty. Water . . . if only he could get a drink of water. He weakened and stumbled and started to crawl. Water . . . he needed water. He saw a figure in the distance and crawled toward it. It was a man with a suitcase.

He crawled to him. "Water!" he cried. "Water! Do you have a drink of water?"

"No. No water," answered the man. "I'm a tie salesman. Do you want to buy a tie?"

"Are you crazy? I'm dying of thirst. What do I need a tie for?"

The man shrugged and walked away.

A couple of hours later, there was the salesman again. "Are you sure you don't want a tie?"

The pilot said, "No tie. What I need is water."

The salesman shrugged again and walked away.

It was getting on toward evening when all of a sudden, on the horizon, in the middle of the barren desert sands, a modern cocktail lounge appeared with neon lights blazing. With his last strength the pilot crawled to the door. There was a uniformed doorman.

"Please. Please . . . I've got to have something to drink," the pilot wailed.

"Sorry, pal," said the doorman, "Nobody's admitted without a tie."

I have an aunt—a schoolteacher—who with a group of other teachers booked a safari trip into the jungles of Africa. They were having a wonderful time, but one of their colleagues, Mabel, a photography bug, kept falling behind snapping this and snapping that.

The guide kept warning her, "Stay with the group. There are all kinds of wild animals out there."

But Mabel kept falling behind. Well, wouldn't you know it, one day as she lagged behind, a gigantic gorilla dropped out of the trees, scooped her up, and disappeared with her into the jungle. For days search parties combed the jungle in vain. No Mabel. Months passed.

Then one day, beaten and bedraggled, Mabel showed up in a clearing. She was rushed to a hospital.

My aunt caught the earliest flight to Africa and hurried to the hospital. There was Mabel in bed, pale and wan.

"Mabel, dear," cried my aunt. "How do you feel?"

Mabel looked up from her bed and in a woebegone voice answered, "How should I feel? Three weeks I'm here, he doesn't phone . . . he doesn't write . . . ."

A handsome young couple were walking down Fifth Avenue in New York. They stopped to look into the window of Tiffany's. "Oh darling," she cooed, "if I only had that diamond brooch, I would be the happiest girl in the world."

"Nothing to it, sweetheart," said the guy. He reached into his trenchcoat and from an inside pocket pulled out a brick, tossed it through the plate glass, pulled out the brooch, and handed it to her.

She kissed him, and they walked on.

A few blocks farther, they came to the Bergdorf-Goodman department store. There in the window was an ankle-length chinchilla coat.

"Oh sugardrop," she purred, "if only I could have that fur coat to go with my brooch, it would make me so-o-o happy."

He looked at her lovingly. "No problem, honeybun." He reached once more inside his coat, pulled out another brick, tossed it through the window, pulled out the coat, shook off the glass, and put it around her.

Once more, she kissed him.

They wandered down to West 57th Street, and there in the window was a Rolls Royce.

"Oh, babykins, with the brooch and the lovely coat and that Rolls, I would be, oh, so ecstatically happy, I . . . ."

"Now, look, Shirley, I'm not made out of bricks!"

It had been raining for three weeks in the Deep South, and the Hoosimiwatsee River overflowed and flooded the valley to the rooftops. There on his roof sat Deacon Frobisher, water up to his ankles. A man in a canoe paddled past and shouted, "Jump in, Deacon, I'll take you to higher ground."

"No, thank you, son," answered the deacon. "I have faith in the Lord. He will save me."

Soon the water was up to the deacon's waist, and a motorboat chugged past. "Hop in, Deacon," called the boatman. "I'll take you to safety."

"No, thanks," the deacon said again. "I have faith in the Lord. He will save me."

An hour later, a helicopter flew overhead. "Hey, Deacon!" called the pilot. "Grab the rope! I'll fly you to higher ground."

"No, thanks," the Deacon called back. "I have faith in the Lord. He will save me."

And off flew the helicopter. The water kept rising. After swimming and treading water for hours, the deacon drowned and, of course, went to Heaven. He finally wangled an interview with his maker.

"You know, Lord, I'm disappointed," he said. "I had such faith that you wouldn't let me down. What happened?"

The Lord looked at him, shook his head, and said, "Hey, what do you want from me? I sent a canoe, a motorboat, and a helicopter!"

A few years ago, three American executives—a manager, a salesman, and an engineer—on a business trip to France were caught in some very serious hanky-panky—serious enough to have them condemned to death by guillotine. The day of the execution arrived, and the three men were led into the place of execution. The executioner told each one he could be beheaded face up or face down.

The manager was first. He chose face up. The executioner pulled the rope and down came the blade. But, miracle of miracles, it stopped just a quarter of an inch from the manager's throat. The executioner told him that by law he could not be subjected to double jeopardy. Therefore, he was set free.

Then came the salesman's turn. "Face up or face down?" he was asked.

"Face up, of course," he responded, snapping his fingers. He took his place.

"Ready . . . set . . . pull!" Down hurtled the blade and again stopped a mere quarter of an inch from the salesman's neck. He, too, was set free.

Then came the engineer's turn. He, too, chose to face the blade. He took his place.

"Ready . . . set . . . ."

Just then the engineer shouted, "Hold it! I think I see the problem . . . . !"

A few months ago, the newly appointed assistant secretary of the Department of Indian Affairs was making his first inspection tour of a western Indian reservation, and, of course, he made a speech. "With this administration," he declaimed, "the American Indian will achieve a new burst of glory."

The response was overwhelming. "Umgawa!" shouted his audience.

Wow! he thought to himself, I've got them going. "With

this administration you will get improved medical service and larger hospitals!''

''Umgawa! Umgawa!'' roared his listeners.

Buoyed up by this response, the bureaucrat continued, ''We want to see every young man and woman getting a college degree.''

Again, the response was overwhelming. ''Umgawa! Umgawa! Umgawa!''

When the politician's address was finished, the chief of the tribe presented him with a beautiful white horse.

As the assistant secretary circled the horse admiringly, the chief cautioned, ''Be careful, sir, and do not step in the umgawa!''

———————

As you know, there is no nut bigger than a golf nut. This is a true story about a friend of mine, Herb. Now he and another friend of mine, Sam, had a golf date every Wednesday for the past ten years. They would tee off early in the morning, be finished about 3:30, go into the clubhouse to wash the dust from their throats, and then go on home to dinner. Their wives were used to the routine and usually had a lovely dinner waiting for them about five.

Well, two weeks ago, Herb left for his usual game. At five o'clock, his wife, Sheila, had his dinner on the table. Five-thirty came—no Herb. ''Traffic,'' she reasoned. Six. Seven. Eight. She was getting really worried. Nine. Ten. Should she call the hospital? Finally at eleven there was a faint tapping at the door. She opened it, and there on the doorstep was Herb, dusty and bedraggled. She pulled him in and kissed him with relief. ''Darling, what happened?''

Half dead, Herb told her, ''What a horrible day this has been. Sam and I were on the third tee when he had a heart attack and died. Since about 10:00 a.m., it's been hit the ball, drag Sam . . . hit the ball, drag Sam . . . hit the ball, drag Sam . . . hit the ball . . . .''

To many people, the game of golf is their greatest passion. I am one of those people, and for years I've been part of a foursome that played religiously every Sunday. We had to play religiously because it was Sunday. Well, one of our group, Sam, passed away and there we were on the prowl to fill his vacancy. Well, this particular Sunday, there was this fellow we knew casually—his name was Steve—and he was moping around the first tee looking at loose ends. We asked him if he'd like to go around with us, and he jumped at the offer.

We were on the seventh green, which runs along Highway 202. Steve was addressing the ball for an eight-foot putt when along the highway came a funeral procession. Steve stood up, turned toward the highway, took his hat off, and bowed his head until the cortege was out of sight. We thought that was very nice, and we told him so.

"Listen," he said, "that's the least I could do. We were married for over twenty years!"

There were three accountants who had such a backlog of work that they decided to come in on a Sunday and try to catch up. Their office was on the sixtieth floor of the Natural Artificial Preservative Building. Wouldn't you know it? The very day they showed up, the elevators were being repaired and the electricity was shut down. There were Lonnie, Marion, and Fred, in a big dilemma.

"I'll tell you what," suggested Fred. "We're here. Let's go through with it. We'll walk up the stairs. Here's what we'll do. Lonnie, you are a great storyteller, you tell funny stories for the first twenty floors. Me, I was in my high school glee club, I'll sing songs for the next twenty, and Marion, you have an ear for drama, you tell us sad stories for the last twenty."

That sounded like a good idea, so off they went. For the first twenty flights, Lonnie kept them in stitches with stories, riddles, and one-liners. Then Fred took over. He sang all the songs made popular by Mel Torme, Frank Sinatra, and Willie Nelson, and before they knew it, they had mounted forty stories.

"Okay, Marion, now it's your turn," Lonnie said.

She looked distraught. Her face puckered up in grief. "I have such a sad story to tell, it's going to really, truly devastate you." She started to weep. "Fellows," she sobbed, "this story is going to break your heart." She sat down on a step and started to cry.

"Come on, kid," urged her two colleagues, "we can take it."

"I hope so," she sobbed. "I forgot to bring the office keys!"

Three well-fed, well-heeled, balding chief executive officers were sipping their cocktails in the lounge of the famed New York Union Club. They were arguing about when you know that you've arrived.

"You've arrived," said Mr. Bigbucks, "when you're sitting in the oval office having an intimate chat with the president of the United States."

"That's only part of it," said Mr. Cashstash. "You've arrived when you're sitting in the oval office having an intimate chat with the president of the United States, and the red phone rings, and the president doesn't pick it up."

"That's almost it," said Mr. Bullioncube. "You know you've arrived when you're sitting in the oval office having an intimate chat with the president of the United States, and the red phone rings. The president picks it up, listens a moment, hands you the phone, and says, "It's for you!"

You've heard about evil people. Bruce Blackheart was the worst! There wasn't a vice he wasn't adept at. There was no atrocity he had not committed. There was no law he hadn't broken. He was bad, bad, bad! Well, Bruce up and died. He had spent a thoroughly interesting life, and he was prepared to pay for his sins. He was in the lobby of the Hereafter office building and there was the elevator. He got in and looked for the down button. There was only one button, and he pressed it. The elevator went up, up, up, and finally deposited him on a pink cloud. In front of him were the solid gold, pearl-studded gates of Heaven.

Must be some sort of a mistake, thought Bruce. To the right of the Pearly Gates was an alabaster marble desk. On a solid gold plaque was inscribed "St. Peter." Next to that, another sign—also solid gold—said, "Out to lunch. Back in an eon. Please be seated and wait." Bruce seated himself on the sofa and picked up a magazine from the coffee table. A back issue, of course. First, he skimmed through *Popular Mechanics*, dated 400,000 B.C., and read an interesting article on a new invention called the wheel. There was a back issue of *Penthouse*, and, since he had always been interested in real estate, he picked it up and skimmed through it. It was dated 5000 B.C., and the centerfold was Eve B.A. (Before Apple).

All of a sudden, he became aware of weeping and wailing coming from the left. He looked over, and in front of this huge granite wall a multitude of all races, all religions, and all sexes were hitting their heads against the wall, trying to kick themselves, and tearing out their hair. It was all very interesting, but Bruce went back to the magazines.

Just then St. Peter returned from his lunch. "Next!" he called.

Bruce went up to the desk. St. Peter handed him a key and pressed a button. The gates swung open. "Welcome to Heaven. Have a nice hereafter," he said.

"Excuse me, sir. There's been some mistake. I'm Bruce Blackheart. I'm bad. I'm evil. I should be going to the other place. Look me up in your record book."

St. Peter smiled. "No mistake. You see, we don't keep records—never have. Everybody goes in."

Bruce shrugged his shoulders, took his key, and started for the gate. He paused. "Excuse me again, St. Peter. I'm very curious. What's going on by that granite wall? Who are those people?"

St. Peter looked at him and grinned. "Oh, them. They're the people who didn't know that we don't keep records!"

A friend of mine was driving down one of the backroads in the Midwest. He was kind of lost, so he pulled over to a farmer working in his front yard to ask directions. As he approached the man, he saw a pig walk past. The pig had a wooden leg. My friend was amazed; he forgot he was lost. "Mister," he asked, "why does your pig have a wooden leg?"

The farmer straightened up and scratched the stubble on his chin. "That pig," he drawled, "that pig ain't no ordinary pig. That pig is a great pig. Let me tell you about that pig. Last Christmas Eve, my wife and I trimmed the Christmas tree and went up to bed. In the middle of the night, the tree caught fire and set the house afire. That pig broke down the door, pulled both my kids, my wife, and me to safety. That's one hell of a pig."

"Yeah, yeah," said my friend. "That's really terrific, but why does that pig have a wooden leg?"

The farmer picked a weed and continued. "That pig is one great pig. My little three-year-old son was lost in the woods. We couldn't find him for eight hours. That pig climbed up a tree and there was my son. He brought him down and back home. Man, that's one special pig!"

"Fantastic!" marveled my friend. "But why does he have a wooden leg?"

"That is a great pig," said the famer. "Just last week I was driving my tractor, and it tipped over into a ditch right on top of me. That pig . . . that pig dug under the tractor and pulled me to safety. That's one great pig."

"I understand," wailed my friend. "He's a very special pig. But for goodness' sake, tell me, why does he have a wooden leg?"

The farmer looked at him gravely and shook his head. "Hey mister, you can't eat a pig like that all at one time!"

The Devil and St. Peter were having a terrible argument. It seems that Satan, with his fire-engine-red Porsche, had knocked a great big hole in the wall that separated Heaven from Hell. St. Peter wanted the hole repaired, and the Devil refused.

"If you don't fix that hole, I'll sue you!" shouted St. Peter.

"Go ahead," answered the Devil. "Where are you going to find a good lawyer in heaven?"

This is a true story. A guy named Hector Deadbeat was up to his eyebrows in debt. He owed everybody. He went to his friend, a chemist, and tried to buy a cyanide capsule. "Why kill yourself?" asked his friend. "I have secretly developed a pill that will put you in a catatonic state. You'll look dead, but you won't be. We'll hold a wake, and when it's over, I'll ship you to some distant city. You'll revive in about five days, and you can start your life all over again."

So Hector took the pill. There he was, laid out handsomely in the funeral parlor. And people were passing the casket to pay their respects.

One of his creditors leaned over the body. "Hector," he said, "why did you do it? You only owed me ten thousand dollars. I could have waited."

Another of his creditors came by. "Hector," he said, weeping, "Hector, for a lousy twenty-five thousand dollars you didn't have to kill yourself. Your friendship meant more to me."

And so it went, creditor after creditor, until up to the coffin came a big, burly guy. "Hector, you dirty rat. You ruined my life. I loaned you one hundred and fifty thousand dollars. You said you'd pay me back in three days. You didn't. I lost my business. I lost my house, and my wife divorced me. I'm going to get even. I'm going to take this butcher knife and stick it in your heart and twist it for every buck you owe me!"

Hector forced open one eye, pointed, and murmured, "You, I'll pay!"

My friend Harry was out driving one day, and he got a flat tire. So he pulled to the side of the road near a ten-foot-high wall in front of an insane asylum. He took his jack from the trunk, jacked up the car, and removed the hubcap and lug nuts. He put the lug nuts in the hubcap and placed it on a nearby sewer grill. While removing the tire, he hit it against the hubcap and down went the lug nuts into the sewer. He had a wire hanger in his car, so he undid it, and there he was on his knees trying to hook the lug nuts with the hook. They were way out of reach.

He sat up in despair. All of a sudden, he heard a "Psst! Psst! Psst!" coming from above. He looked up, and there, with his elbows on top of the brick wall, was this man wearing a Napoleon hat.

"What's your problem?" asked the inmate.

Harry explained his predicament.

"Listen," said the inmate. "Take one lug from each of your other three wheels, put them on the wheel with the missing nuts, and you'll be able to drive safely to the nearest garage."

My friend did just that. When he had the lug nuts in place, he looked up at the man on the wall and thanked him. "How is it," he asked, "that a person like you is in there?"

The man grinned down at him and said, "I'm crazy, not stupid!"

The president of Israel, on a state visit to the United States, was sitting in the oval office chatting with our president. He noticed on the president's desk, beside a battery of black phones, a red phone, a white one, and a blue one.

He looked at the president. "Those colored phones. What are they for?" he asked.

"Well," explained the president, "the red one is the hot line to the Kremlin. The white one is my direct line to the legislature, and that blue one is my direct line to God."

"How convenient," said the Israeli. "Listen, I have an urgent need to talk to God. Do you mind if I use the blue phone?"

"I personally wouldn't mind," answered the president, "but we are on a very tight budget right now."

"I will gladly pay for the call," said the Israeli.

The president told him to go ahead. After a brief call, he asked our president, "How much is that?"

The president pulled a phone book out of his top desk drawer. "Let's see," he murmured. "Four minutes, Washington to God. That'll be four hundred ninety-two dollars and seventy-three cents."

The president of Israel wrote the United States president a check.

About a year and a half later our president went on a state visit to Israel. He and his old friend were sitting in the presidential palace shooting the breeze, and our president noticed that the Israeli also had a blue phone. "Hey," said he, "I just happen to have to talk to God real badly. Do you mind if I use your phone?"

"Go ahead," said his host.

After a brief conversation, our president asked, "How much do I owe you?"

"Twenty-five cents," was the reply.

"Only twenty-five cents? How come?"

"In Israel, calling God is a local call!"

A friend of mine had been to an office party and came home about 2:00 a.m. There was his lovely wife in bed gently snoring. He went to the bathroom, got two aspirin and a glass of water, and came back. He shook her awake and handed her the aspirin.

"What's this?" she asked.

"Two aspirin," he answered.

"But I don't have a headache," she grumbled.

"Terrific," he came back. "Move over."

A busload of churchwomen was going to a convention when the bus was struck by a train and all of the passengers were killed. Of course, they went straight to Heaven. But they weren't expected yet. None of them were scheduled to be there for at least another twenty-five years. St. Peter didn't have sufficient accommodations for them. He prevailed upon the Devil to put them up in Hell temporarily while he built some new apartments. The Devil grudgingly agreed.

Hardly two months had passed by when the Devil came tearing into St. Peter's office. "Get those women out of Hell!" he screamed. "I want them out! Immediately!"

"Why? What can forty churchwomen do to upset you so? They're quite harmless."

"Harmless? They've been here only two months, and what with the rummage sales, the cake bakes, the chicken dinners, and the amateur theatricals, they've raised a fortune in money and plan to put in air conditioning!"

It was a sad, sad day. Herbert's wife was dying of a terminal disease. Her hours were numbered. She lay there and sighed. "We've had a good life, Herbert. Fifteen blissful years. You are the kind of man who needs a good woman. I want you to promise me that after I go, you will marry again."

"I'll try," he choked.

"Herbert, I want her to have my violet Lincoln Continental with the leather upholstery."

"Yes, dear," he answered.

"And, Herbert, I want you to give her my mink coat trimmed in sable with the sealskin lining."

"Yes, dear," he sobbed.

"And, Herbert, give her my full set of gold-plated golf clubs."

He looked at her mournfully and said, "I can't do that . . . she's left-handed!"

SOURCE MATERIAL

There are many collections of jokes that can be borrowed from your public library. Several magazines, like *Reader's Digest*, feature a joke section.

FIVE CHECK-POINTS OF GREAT SPEAKING: A TEAR SHEET FOR YOUR POCKET

5 CHECK POINTS OF GREAT SPEAKING

☐ **TARGET**
Set your objective
(TARGET) and go
for the bull's-eye

☐ **ENERGY**
Glowing will give
you enthusiasm,
personality and
projection

☐ **EYEBALL**
Talk to each person,
one at a time—
eyeball to eyeball

☐ **HARD OF HEARING**
Talk as if each person is
hard of hearing—for better
diction, voice projection
and believable delivery

☐ **LOVE**
Love your audience
for warmth, sincerity
and credibility

INDEX

REFERENCES

Quotations used throughout *The How-To of Great Speaking* are taken from the following sources:

John Barton, *Playing Shakespeare* (New York: Methuen, Inc., 1984).

Ira Berkow, Sugar Ray Leonard story, *New York Times,* reprinted with permission from *Reader's Digest* (May 1984).

Leo Buscaglia, *Loving and Learning* (New York: Fawcett Columbine, 1982).

Toby Cole and Helen Krish Chinoy, *Actors on Acting* (New York: Crown Publishing, 1970).

Clare Colvin, "As You Like It or Not," *Drama 1986.*

Jennifer Dunning, "The New American Actor," *New York Times Magazine* (October 1983).

Clifton Fadiman (ed.), *The Little, Brown Book of Anecdotes* (Boston: Little, Brown, 1985).

Lewis Funke and John E. Booth, *Actors Talk about Acting* (New York: Random House, 1961).

Rita Gam, *Actress to Actress: Memories, Profiles, Conversations* (New York: Nick Lyons Books, 1986).

Ruth Gordon, *An Open Book* (Garden City: Doubleday and Company, 1980).

Dag Hammarskjold, *Markings* (New York: Alfred A. Knopf, 1964).

Robert Lewis, *Method or Madness* (New York: Samuel French, Inc., 1958).

Eva Mekler, *The New Generation of Acting Teachers* (New York: Viking, 1987).

Helen Ormsbee, *Backstage with Actors: From the Time of Shakespeare to the Present Day* (New York: Benjamin Blom, 1969).

Susan Shacter and Don Shewey, *Caught in the Act: New York Actors Face to Face* (New York: New American Library, 1986).

William Shakespeare, *Hamlet,* in *The Works of William Shakespeare Gathered into One Volume* (New York: Oxford University Press, Shakespeare Head Press Edition, 1938).

Constantin Stanislavsky, *An Actor Prepares,* translated by Elizabeth Reynolds Hagwood, (New York: New York Theatre Arts Books, 1948).

William C. Young, *Famous Actors and Actresses on the American Stage: Documents of American Theatre History* (New York: R. R. Bowker, 1975).

ABOUT THE AUTHORS

Hal Persons

For over twenty years, Hal Persons has trained a host (he stopped counting at 45,000) of executives to speak with style and grace in the board room, at sales presentations, or on television appearances. His specialty is banishing butterflies—the butterflies that can turn a brilliant person into a stilted puppet. He has conducted his "Personal Communications Workshop" at Fortune 500 companies such as AT&T, IBM, Chase Manhattan Bank, and Hill and Knowlton.

His strength is helping a speaker be natural, powerful, and charismatic. He wishes he could claim that he invented his method, but the technique he uses was introduced by William Shakespeare and communicated by word of mouth to Constantin Stanislovsky. In other words, Hal goes to the source of effective speaking—he teaches theatrical performance skills to executives.

A fortunate amalgam of business, educational, and theatrical skills made his Personal Communications Institute possible. Before its organization in 1967, Hal Persons had a career in advertising and conducted a highly successful professional theatre school, The Theatre Academy. He had also produced and directed television shows on NBC, CBS, and Mutual. He spent many years as director, actor, and stage manager on Broadway, in national touring shows, and in summer stock companies.

Hal has taught verbal communications skills at Columbia University Graduate School of Business, the American Institute of Banking, and at York and LaGuardia Colleges.

For more information about scheduling one of Hal Person's workshops call or write:

Personal Communications Institute
48-05 Browvale Avenue
Flushing, NY 11362
718/229-3254

Lianne Mercer

Lianne Mercer has taught interpersonal and interviewing skills at the University of Michigan, San Jacinto Junior College, and Texas Women's University. In association with a leading writing consulting firm, she has taught business and technical writing at several Fortune 500 companies. She is a writing consultant, psychiatric nurse, and poet.

Lianne has written numerous magazine articles and has co-authored a textbook, *Fundamental Skills in the Nurse-Patient Relationship*, with Patricia O'Connor, PhD. (Philadelphia: W. B. Saunders, Co., 1969, 2nd Edition, 1974).